# ELFQUEST

## STARGAZER'S
## HUNT

D1228104

# ELFQUEST™

## STARGAZER'S HUNT

**VOLUME TWO**

STORY BY
**WENDY** AND **RICHARD PINI**

SCRIPT AND LAYOUTS BY
**WENDY PINI**

ART AND COLORS BY
**SONNY STRAIT**

LETTERS BY
**NATE PIEKOS** OF **BLAMBOT®**

COVER BY
**WENDY PINI**

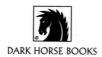

DARK HORSE BOOKS

PUBLISHER **MIKE RICHARDSON**
EDITOR **RACHEL ROBERTS**
ASSOCIATE EDITOR **JENNY BLENK**
ASSISTANT EDITOR **ANASTACIA FERRY**
COLLECTION DESIGNER **SKYLER WEISSENFLUH**
DIGITAL ART TECHNICIAN **ALLYSON HALLER**

NEIL HANKERSON Executive Vice President • TOM WEDDLE Chief Financial Officer • DALE LAFOUNTAIN Chief Information Officer • TIM WIESCH Vice President of Licensing • MATT PARKINSON Vice President ofMarketing • VANESSA TODD-HOLMES Vice President of Production and Scheduling • MARK BERNARDI Vice President of Book Trade and Digital Sales • RANDY LAHRMAN Vice President of Product Development • KEN LIZZI General Counsel • DAVE MARSHALL Editor in Chief • DAVEY ESTRADA Editorial Director • CHRIS WARNER Senior Books Editor • CARY GRAZZINI Director of Specialty Projects • LIA RIBACCHI Art Director • MATT DRYER Director of Digital Art and Prepress • MICHAEL GOMBOS Senior Director of Licensed Publications KARI YADRO Director of Custom Programs • KARI TORSON Director of International Licensing

Published by Dark Horse Books
A division of Dark Horse Comics LLC
10956 SE Main Street
Milwaukie, OR 97222

DarkHorse.com
Comic Shop Locator Service: Comicshoplocator.com

First edition: May 2022
eBOOK ISBN 978-1-50672-142-2
ISBN 978-1-50672-141-5

1 3 5 7 9 10 8 6 4 2
Printed in China

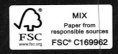

**ELFQUEST: STARGAZER'S HUNT VOLUME TWO**

ElfQuest® © 2020, 2021, 2022 Warp Graphics, Inc. ElfQuest, its logos, characters, situations, all related indicia, and their distinctive likenesses are trademarks of Warp Graphics, Inc. All rights reserved. Dark Horse Books® and the Dark Horse logo are registered trademarks of Dark Horse Comics LLC. All rights reserved. No portion of this publication may be reproduced or transmitted, in any form or by any means, without the express written permission of Dark Horse Comics LLC. Names, characters, places, and incidents featured in this publication either are the product of the author's imagination or are used fictitiously. Any resemblance to actual persons (living or dead), events, institutions, or locales, without satiric intent, is coincidental.

This book collects *ElfQuest: Stargazer's Hunt* #5–#8.

Library of Congress Cataloging-in-Publication Data

Names: Pini, Wendy, author, cover artist. | Pini, Richard, author. |
    Strait, Sonny, artist. | Piekos, Nate, letterer.
Title: ElfQuest : stargazer's hunt / story by Wendy and Richard Pini ; art
    by Sonny Strait ; letters by Nate Piekos ; cover by Wendy Pini.
Other titles: Stargazer's hunt
Description: First edition. | Milwaukie, OR : Dark Horse Books, 2021- |
    "This book collects ElfQuest: Stargazer's Hunt #1-#4." | Summary: "When
    ElfQuest: The Final Quest concluded, it ended the hero's journey of
    Cutter Kinseeker, chief of the Wolfriders. But that was only the start
    of a new adventure for Cutter's "brother in all but blood," Skywise. Now
    the stargazer elf, who thought he knew everything about Cutter,
    discovers how mistaken he was. In times past, whenever he has felt lost
    or empty, he has turned to the starry skies for guidance. Now is no
    exception. Once again Skywise sets his sights on the cosmic horizon for
    answers, sending him on his own epic quest from the elves' ancestral
    Star Home through uncharted space, and back to the World of Two Moons"--
    Provided by publisher.
Identifiers: LCCN 2020046084 (print) | LCCN 2020046085 (ebook) | ISBN
    9781506714769 (v. 1 ; trade paperback) | ISBN 9781506719603 (v. 1 ;
    ebook)
Subjects: LCSH: Comic books, strips, etc.
Classification: LCC PN6728 .E45 P5637 2021 (print) | LCC PN6728 .E45
    (ebook) | DDC 741.5/973--dc23
LC record available at https://lccn.loc.gov/2020046084
LC ebook record available at https://lccn.loc.gov/2020046085

# FOUND IN THE STARS
by Wendy Pini

Every serious *ElfQuest* fan knows that Cutter Kinseeker is my avatar, just as Skywise is Richard's. Cutter is my personal voice in the *ElfQuest* saga. He speaks for me, and Skywise has always fulfilled that role for Richard.

But, as the writer of most of the series, I must remain as true to Skywise's nature and personality as I was to Cutter's. The relationship between Cutter and Skywise—that love story—was **the** cord connecting all the vertebrae in the tale's backbone. Were that dynamic ever to be mishandled, no other part of the epic skeleton would function.

This is why Richard's input has been essential throughout the telling of *ElfQuest* from start to finish. It was to him I turned for answers when I needed to ask, "How would Skywise say this?" or "What would he do here?" Sometimes I found my own guesses were off the mark, or outright wrong. The surprising and ingenious solution Richard offered to a difficult Skywise moment often sparked whole new scenes that weren't in the original draft.

Although we celebrate our fiftieth wedding anniversary in 2022, I've never been able to second-guess this mysterious, mercurial man in our day-to-day lives. So why, then, should I be able to intuit Skywise's every thought and movement as expertly as I know Cutter's? Cutter is **me**. I know me pretty well. But even after all these years, Richard and I still discover new things about each other. And everything I've come to know about my wonderfully unpredictable lifemate has gone into enriching Skywise as a character.

Which brings me to the long-awaited *Stargazer's Hunt* series—the conclusion of which you now hold in your (hopefully) eager hands. From the get-go, I felt a deep obligation to do as much justice to Skywise's hero's journey, in the aftermath of his soul brother's death, as I had done for Cutter in *The Final Quest*. The outline of this coda was imagined (and hinted at) by Richard and me more than two decades ago. But when it came time to send Skywise on his own quest, we knew the story had to be told from **his** perspective. This was not a viewpoint I was accustomed to shining a bright light on. How do you elevate one from "companion to the champion" to the role of "hero"?

Always the Wolfrider chief's ideal sidekick, Skywise must come into his own—must deal with Cutter's death and the loss of that comfortable, loving relationship. That is what launches him on his journey through the stars, destination unknown. Even as you, gentle reader, discovered Skywise's innermost thoughts and fears in volume 1, I came to know him and identify with him more than I ever had before. Occasionally a source of comic relief, a deep thinker, philosopher, and star explorer, he always wished to come into sharp focus. Out from under Cutter's shadow, he proved himself to be altogether his own person.

Helped immensely by my assistant and spiritual twin **Sonny Strait** (whose favorite elf has always been Skywise), the artwork took on a fresh, expansive style that truly fit the tone of the story. Sonny expressed his spiritual side most in depictions of the Starhome. We often joked that we were trying to tell a story about heaven, yet keep it full of conflict and pathos. Somehow we managed it. Here you will encounter what I consider the finest work Sonny and I have done together. We went deep into the spirit realm with the full intent of taking you along.

What mattered most, of course, was that Richard be satisfied with our efforts. Without gushing, he in his own way responded, "Perfect!" and we all heaved sighs of relief. The ordeal was over, for Skywise and for us.

In my opinion, *Stargazer's Hunt* is unique among fantasy-adventure comic series. It contains no violence, except what is natural in the wild. No one wantonly hurts anyone, for healing and reconciliation must be the elixir with which Skywise, the hero, returns home. Does he? See—and decide—for yourself. Richard, Sonny, and I have completed this journey and have put our pens down and our feet up . . . for now.

MOMENTS AGO, SKYWISE'S BOTTOMLESS CURIOSITY FOUND THE BOTTOM OF A RABBIT HOLE!
WHAT'S THIS?
LOOK AT HIS EYES!
THOSE ARE THE EYES OF A HIGH ONE--OR I'LL GO UP AND SUCK TOPSIDE AIR!
BRZZRT BLIT BLIT!
Y-YOU KNOW ABOUT HIGH ONES?
??!
OF COURSE WE DO.
ARE YOU A SURVIVOR? IF SO, IT'S A WONDER!

BEWILDERED BY THE QUESTION, SKYWISE ALLOWS HIMSELF TO BE LED DOWN, DOWN, AND DOWN--
--INTO AN UNDERGROUND DOMAIN AS IMPOSING, IN ITS WAY, AS THE ECHOING HALLS OF BLUE MOUNTAIN IN ITS PRIME--
--YET BUSTLING WITH VIBRANT ACTIVITY AND LIFE.
I DON'T GET WHAT YOU MEAN BY "SURVIVOR." BUT I SURE HAD TO SURVIVE THE ROTTEN AIR OUTSIDE!
AS HAVE WE ALL, AT ONE TIME OR ANOTHER.
FANCY-FANCY BIG ROOM!
BUZZ-BUZZ-THINGS LOOK LIKE THISTLECAP, BUT NOT!
WE'LL DO OUR BEST TO MAKE YOU WELCOME IN OUR SAFE HAVEN.
BEFORE WE CELEBRATE YOU AS YOU DESERVE--
--LET US SHOW YOU HOW WE REMEMBER OUR GRACIOUS HIGH ONES!
GASP! IT'S TRUE!
OTHER VESSELS FROM THE ONCE-DYING STARHOME DID REACH OTHER WORLDS!

THE SURVIVOR'S ACCENT! STRANGE HOW HE SEEMS TO GROWL SOME OF HIS WORDS!
I RATHER LIKE IT!
BZZZRT?!
BA-BLIT! BA-BLIT! BA-BLIT!
THAT'S A HIGH ONE, ALL RIGHT! IN ANCIENT FORM, BEFORE ANY SHAPE-CHANGES.
YOU MEAN CHANGES...TO LOOK LIKE YOU?
"I'LL SHOW YOU," SKYWISE GRINS.

OF COURSE I MAY NEVER DO THIS TRICK--
--SO WELL AS MY LIFEMATE, TIMMAIN!
BUT YOU CAN CHANGE SHAPE! AND YOU CAN FLOAT!
WE NEED SEE NO MORE! YOU ARE A HIGH ONE!
GASP! OOOOOH!
AAAAHHH!
AND WE SCULPERS ARE OVERJOYED THAT YOU'VE COME!
"SCULPERS," EH? ON MY BIRTH-WORLD--
--YOU HAVE COUSINS WHO CALL THEMSELVES TROLLS!
AND MY KIND ARE CALLED ELVES. WE HAVE MANY SIZES AND SHAPES.
"I ARRIVED HERE SMALL... LIKE THE WOLFRIDERS, THE TRIBEMATES I LEFT BEHIND."
LEETAH, OUR LOCK-SEND IS TOO MUCH TO BEAR! I MUST BREAK AWAY!
YOU KNEW CUTTER WAS MORTAL--
--THAT YOU WOULD OUTLIVE HIM--
--YET YOU CHOSE TO BE WITH HIM!

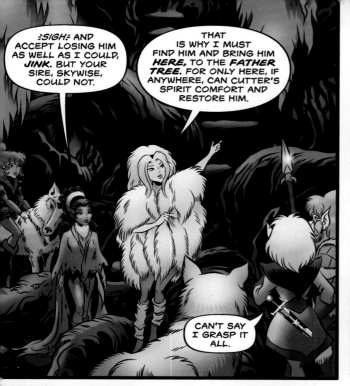

≈SIGH≈ AND ACCEPT LOSING HIM AS WELL AS I COULD, *JINK.* BUT YOUR SIRE, SKYWISE, COULD NOT.

THAT IS WHY I MUST FIND HIM AND BRING HIM *HERE,* TO THE *FATHER TREE,* FOR ONLY HERE, IF ANYWHERE, CAN CUTTER'S SPIRIT COMFORT AND RESTORE HIM.

CAN'T SAY I GRASP IT ALL.

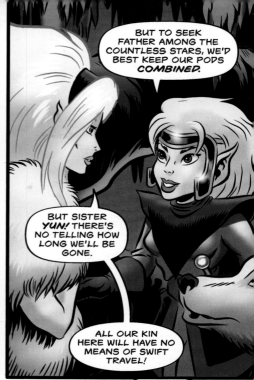

BUT TO SEEK FATHER AMONG THE COUNTLESS STARS, WE'D BEST KEEP OUR PODS *COMBINED.*

BUT SISTER *YUN!* THERE'S NO TELLING HOW LONG WE'LL BE GONE.

ALL OUR KIN HERE WILL HAVE NO MEANS OF SWIFT TRAVEL!

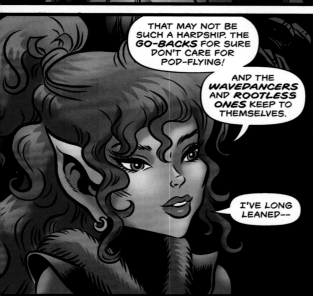

THAT MAY NOT BE SUCH A HARDSHIP. THE *GO-BACKS* FOR SURE DON'T CARE FOR POD-FLYING!

AND THE *WAVEDANCERS* AND *ROOTLESS ONES* KEEP TO THEMSELVES.

I'VE LONG LEANED--

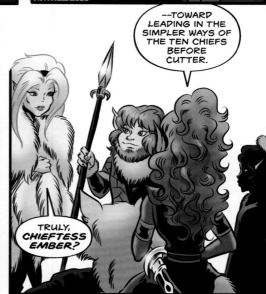

--TOWARD LEADING IN THE SIMPLER WAYS OF THE TEN CHIEFS BEFORE CUTTER.

TRULY, *CHIEFTESS EMBER?*

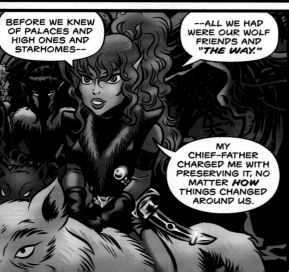

BEFORE WE KNEW OF PALACES AND HIGH ONES AND STARHOMES--

--ALL WE HAD WERE OUR WOLF FRIENDS AND *"THE WAY."*

MY CHIEF-FATHER CHARGED ME WITH PRESERVING IT, NO MATTER *HOW* THINGS CHANGED AROUND US.

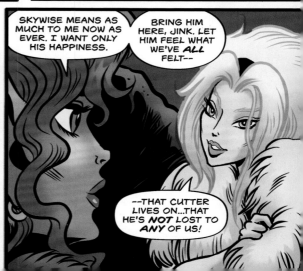

SKYWISE MEANS AS MUCH TO ME NOW AS EVER. I WANT ONLY HIS HAPPINESS.

BRING HIM HERE, JINK. LET HIM FEEL WHAT WE'VE *ALL* FELT--

--THAT CUTTER LIVES ON...THAT HE'S *NOT* LOST TO *ANY* OF US!

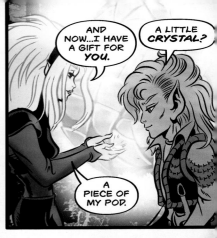

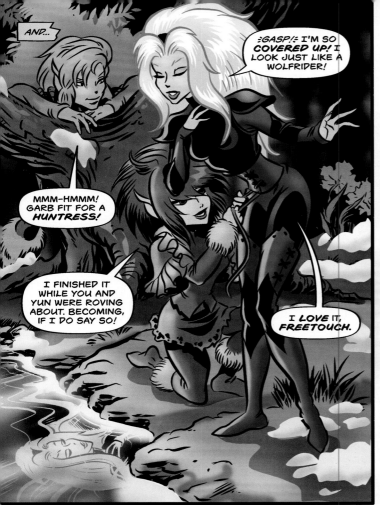

AND...

≥GASP!≤ I'M SO *COVERED UP!* I LOOK JUST LIKE A *WOLFRIDER!*

MMM-HMMM! GARB FIT FOR A *HUNTRESS!*

I FINISHED IT WHILE YOU AND YUN WERE ROVING ABOUT. BECOMING, IF I DO SAY SO!

I *LOVE* IT, *FREETOUCH.*

AND NOW...I HAVE A GIFT FOR *YOU.*

A LITTLE *CRYSTAL?*

A PIECE OF MY POD.

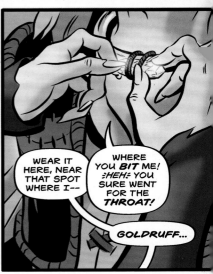

WEAR IT HERE, NEAR THAT SPOT WHERE I--

WHERE YOU *BIT* ME! ≥HEH≤ YOU SURE WENT FOR THE *THROAT!*

GOLDRUFF...

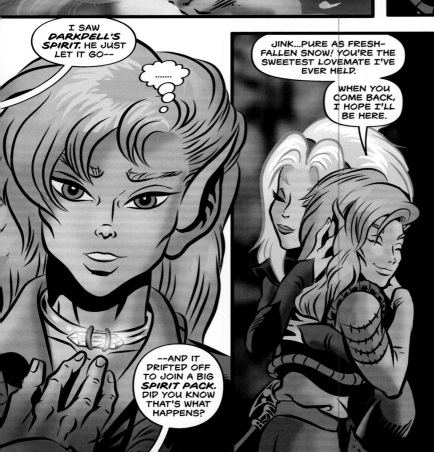

I SAW *DARKDELL'S SPIRIT.* HE JUST LET IT GO--

........

--AND IT DRIFTED OFF TO JOIN A BIG *SPIRIT PACK.* DID YOU KNOW THAT'S WHAT HAPPENS?

JINK...PURE AS FRESH-FALLEN SNOW! YOU'RE THE SWEETEST LOVEMATE I'VE EVER HELD.

WHEN YOU COME BACK, I HOPE I'LL BE HERE.

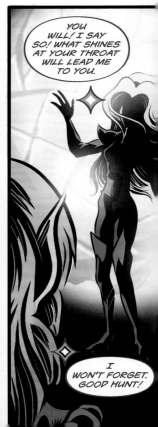

YOU WILL! I SAY SO! WHAT SHINES AT YOUR THROAT WILL LEAD ME TO YOU.

I WON'T FORGET. GOOD HUNT!

WAIT! WAIT!
PRINCESS TRINKET!
KING PICKNOSE WILL HAVE MY NUGGETS IF YOU--
YOU CAAAN'T GO WITHOUT ME!
MY FOLK SAY NO TO EVERYTHING A MAIDEN WANTS TO DO!
I CAN'T LIVE BY THEIR STUFFY OLD RULES ANYMORE!
I-I'LL GO MAD! I'LL RUN WILD!
PLEEEEZE! TAKE ME WITH YOU!
THERE, THERE...
DID YOU THINK WE WOULD REFUSE YOU?
"NO" IS A WORD THE STARS DON'T UNDER-STAND.
SNIFF SNIFF I WAS SCARED YOU WOULD.
PRINCESS!
TELL EVERYONE FARE WELL! I'M GOING TO TRAVEL FAR! SEE THINGS! BE WHAT I WANT!
IN ONE TIME AND PLACE, PARTINGS...

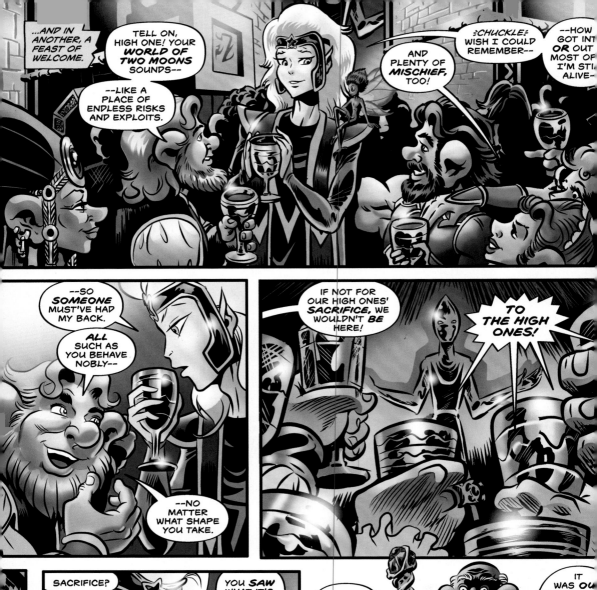

...AND IN ANOTHER, A FEAST OF WELCOME.

TELL ON, HIGH ONE! YOUR *WORLD OF TWO MOONS* SOUNDS--

--LIKE A PLACE OF ENDLESS RISKS AND EXPLOITS.

AND PLENTY OF *MISCHIEF,* TOO!

:CHUCKLE: WISH I COULD REMEMBER--

--HOW GOT INT *OR* OUT MOST OF I'M STI ALIVE-

--SO *SOMEONE* MUST'VE HAD MY BACK.

*ALL* SUCH AS YOU BEHAVE NOBLY--

--NO MATTER WHAT SHAPE YOU TAKE.

IF NOT FOR OUR HIGH ONES' *SACRIFICE,* WE WOULDN'T *BE* HERE!

*TO THE HIGH ONES!*

SACRIFICE?

YOU *SAW* WHAT IT'S LIKE UP THERE.

*TERRIBLE!*

JUST SO, HONORED GUEST.

IT WAS OU NATURE, THE DYIN STARHOME ROOT ABO ONLY I SOIL AN STONE

"BUT GENERATION AFTER GENERATION IN OUR SHARED CRYSTALLINE VESSEL--

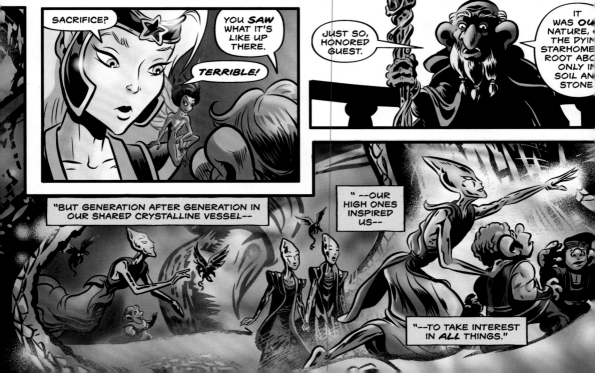

" --OUR HIGH ONES INSPIRED US--

"--TO TAKE INTEREST IN *ALL* THINGS."

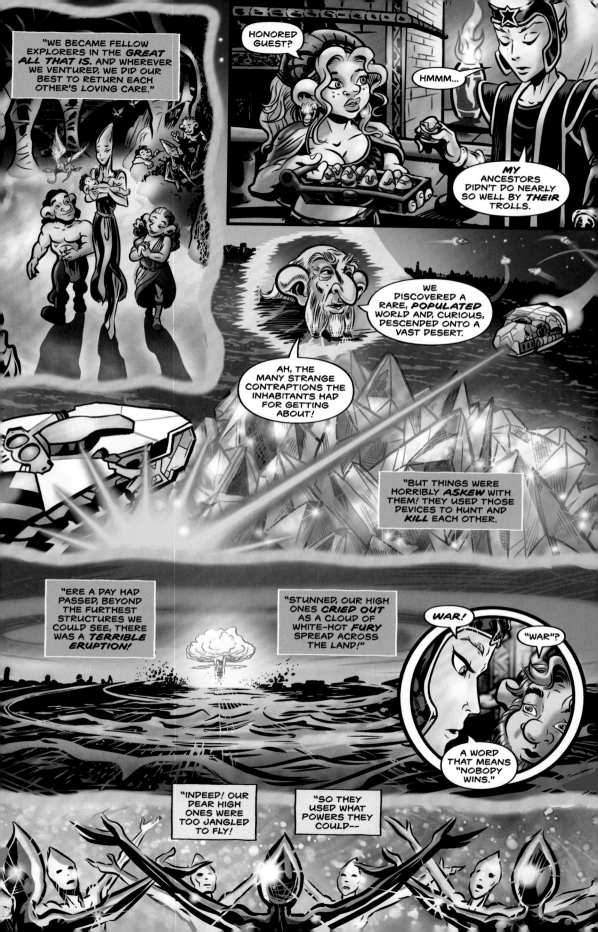

"WE BECAME FELLOW EXPLORERS IN THE *GREAT ALL THAT IS.* AND WHEREVER WE VENTURED, WE DID OUR BEST TO RETURN EACH OTHER'S LOVING CARE."

HONORED GUEST?

HMMM...

*MY* ANCESTORS DIDN'T DO NEARLY SO WELL BY *THEIR* TROLLS.

WE DISCOVERED A RARE, *POPULATED* WORLD AND, CURIOUS, DESCENDED ONTO A VAST DESERT.

AH, THE MANY STRANGE CONTRAPTIONS THE INHABITANTS HAD FOR GETTING ABOUT!

"BUT THINGS WERE HORRIBLY *ASKEW* WITH THEM! THEY USED THOSE DEVICES TO HUNT AND *KILL* EACH OTHER.

"ERE A DAY HAD PASSED, BEYOND THE FURTHEST STRUCTURES WE COULD SEE, THERE WAS A *TERRIBLE ERUPTION!*

"STUNNED, OUR HIGH ONES *CRIED OUT* AS A CLOUD OF WHITE-HOT *FURY* SPREAD ACROSS THE LAND!"

WAR!

"WAR"?

A WORD THAT MEANS "NOBODY WINS."

"INDEED! OUR DEAR HIGH ONES WERE TOO JANGLED TO FLY!

"SO THEY USED WHAT POWERS THEY COULD--

"--TO SWIFTLY CREATE A SHELTER DEEP BENEATH THE FLOOR.
"IN THEIR LOVE FOR US, THEY HURRIED *US* DOWN FIRST.
"BUT BEFORE THEY TOO COULD DESCEND, THERE CAME A SECOND, DEAFENING EXPLOSION--
"--*MUCH* CLOSER... A WAVE OF SEARING HEAT BEYOND DESCRIPTION!
"OUR VESSEL *MELTED!*
"AND OUR HIGH ONES--ALL THANKS BE TO THEIR SPIRITS--WERE *CONSUMED!*
"BUT WE SCULPERS WERE SAFE UNDERGROUND."
EVERY PASSING YEAR, THIS MOONLESS WORLD'S BONES GIVE A *SHRUG*. THAT'S HOW WE MEASURE TIME.
EIGHT EIGHTS TIMES FOUR HAVE WE FELT THOSE TREMORS. IT'S TAKEN THAT LONG TO BUILD OUR REALM.
BUT THERE'S A *SUN* ABOVE WHOSE WARMTH WE'VE NEVER KNOWN. WE MISS BREATHING OPEN AIR THAT NEEDS NO FILTER.
MORE THAN THAT, WE MISS SAILING THE STARS...EXPLORING... *LEARNING!*
"LEARNING." THE ONLY THING THAT SCRATCHES THE ITCH WE ALL HAVE.
*LISTEN!* TAKE ME BACK UP INTO YOUR MELTED SHIP.

"I CAN FLOAT UP, NEAR TO WHERE MY POD PERCHES OUTSIDE, ABOVE THE CEILING.

"MY THOUGHTS CAN REACH IT... *CHANGE* IT--

"--SHAPE IT TO SEND OUT A POWERFUL *CALL*--A HUM JUST LIKE THE STARHOME'S OWN--

"--REACHING EVERYWHERE, THROUGHOUT THE GREAT ALL THAT IS.

"WITH LUCK AND PATIENCE, IN TIME, IT MAY CALL *MORE* OF MY KIND TO YOU.

"FOR ALL WE KNOW, OTHER HIGH ONES' VESSELS ARE *STILL* SOARING FAR AND WIDE.

"IF THEY *DO* COME, I HOPE THEY'RE AS GOOD TO YOU AS THOSE WHO DIED SO YOU COULD LIVE.

"--FOR TROLLS AND ELVES TO EXCHANGE FRIENDSHIP, LET ALONE THE LOVE *YOU* KNEW.

"YOU SEE, ON THE WORLD OF TWO MOONS, IT TOOK A *MOUNTAIN'S AGE*--

"HOW MUCH TIME HAS PASSED *THERE*, I WONDER, SINCE I LEFT IT?"

YOUNG ARCHAEOLOGIST PAR TOLFSSON REINS IN HIS MOUNT, PAUSING AT THE BORDER OF THE INSECT TRIBES' SACRED LAND.
THE TWO WAXING MOONS GRIN DOWN UPON HIM THINLY--
--AS COUNTLESS CRAWLING AND FLYING THINGS CROON THEIR NIGHTLY SONG.
BRRR-UPP BRRR-UPP
DAMN!
BRRROOOOMMMM!
WE'VE CREATED A WORLD OF NOISE AND CONFUSION THAT THEY COULD ONLY WANT TO HIDE FROM.
BUT HAVE WE ALREADY DRIVEN THEM AWAY ALTOGETHER?
EERIE, MANTID-FEATURED TOTEMS WARN, "COME NO FURTHER."
HIS EVERY PRIOR BID FOR TRIBAL CONSENT REFUSED, HE KNOWS HE TRESPASSES NOW.

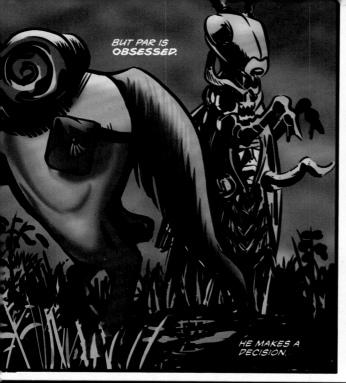

BUT PAR IS *OBSESSED.*

HE MAKES A DECISION.

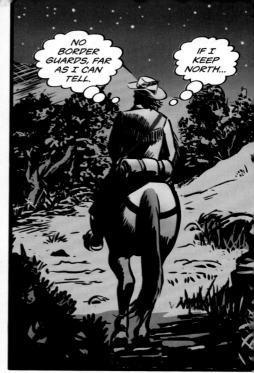

NO BORDER GUARDS, FAR AS I CAN TELL.

IF I KEEP NORTH...

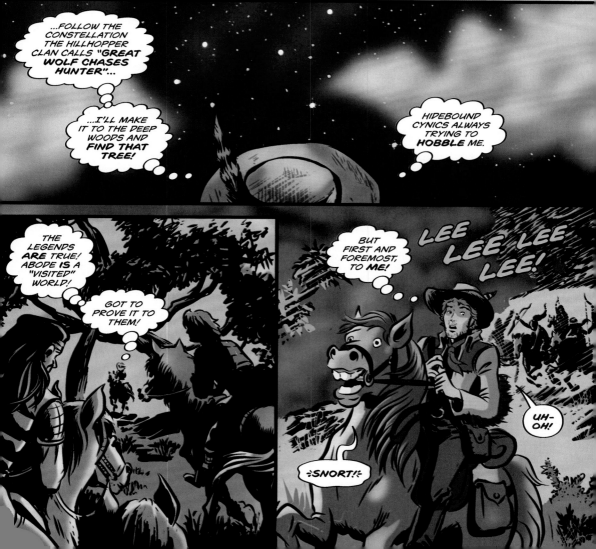

...FOLLOW THE CONSTELLATION THE HILLHOPPER CLAN CALLS *"GREAT WOLF CHASES HUNTER"*...

...I'LL MAKE IT TO THE DEEP WOODS AND FIND THAT TREE!

HIDEBOUND CYNICS ALWAYS TRYING TO *HOBBLE* ME.

THE LEGENDS *ARE* TRUE! ABODE *IS* A "VISITED" WORLD!

GOT TO PROVE IT TO THEM!

BUT FIRST AND FOREMOST, TO *ME!*

LEE LEE LEE LEE!

UH-OH!

≑SNORT!≑

LEE LEE
LEE LEE
LEE LEE LEE!
WHEEEE-OUGH!
HUNN-HUNN-HUNH!
EASY NOW, SWARM! EASY! HEH HEH I KNOW...I KNOW...
YOU KNOW THE LAW, BORDER CRASHER?
THEN WHY DON'T YOU RESPECT IT?
BELIEVE ME, I DO! BUT IF YOU'D JUST...
GASP!

ZAZAPAT IKOPEK!
QUEEN BEE! I-I NEVER THOUGHT I'D HAVE THE HONOR--
TICK-RASH, YOU NOSY GRUB!
LEAVE NOW AND YOU WON'T BE FINED--
--OR JAILED.
MA'AM, I MAY BE JUST A PASTY-FACED "GRUB" TO YOU, BUT I'M GONNA SAY THIS ANYWAY.
I KNOW SOMETHING--SOMEONE NOT HUMAN--ONCE LIVED HERE!
YOU KNOW IT, TOO!
FOR LONG MOMENTS THE IMPOSING MATRIARCH FIXES HIM WITH AN APPRAISING STARE.
THEN...
BACK OFF, SCOUTS. RELAX. HAVE A SMOKE.
HE'S A PESKY FLEA--
--BUT NOT LIKE MOST WE'VE HAD TO BRUSH OFF.
THANK YOU. THIS MEANS EVERYTHING.
DON'T BE TOO SURE. I HAVEN'T DECIDED WHAT "THIS" IS YET.
"SO, GRUB, YOU'VE SPENT YEARS STUDYING THE INSECT TRIBES' LEGENDS. HOW MUCH HAVE YOU PIECED TOGETHER?"

I KNOW THAT A LONG WAY FROM HERE THERE'S AN ANCIENT, DENSE WOOD--
"--AND A STRANGE TREE, TALLER THAN ALL THE REST.
"I SAW IT ONCE, FROM A SMALL PLANE. I KNOW, I KNOW...ILLEGAL FLYOVER. BUT THAT TREE HOLDS SECRETS I'D GIVE MY RIGHT ARM TO LEARN!"
PLEASE, MA'AM, I COME WITH OPEN HANDS. YOU'RE THE ONLY ONE WHO CAN GRANT ME SAFE PASSAGE.
I'VE GOT TO KNOW! THE "HIDDEN ONES"...DO THEY STILL EXIST ON ABODE?
FOR THOSE TRAVELING AT POD-FLIGHT SPEED, TIME DOES NOT PASS AS IT DOES FOR PLANET-BOUND CREATURES.
JINK AND YUN CANNOT TELL IF THEY HAVE JOURNEYED A FEW DAYS...OR MANY EIGHTS OF YEARS.
THEIR FIDGETY TROLL COMPANION, HOWEVER, CAN THINK ONLY OF--

FOOD! OW I YEARN FOR THE TASTE OF IT!
BUT I COULDN'T EAT A BITE! WHY?
YOU SAID WE NEEDED NO SUPPLIES, JINK.
CAN WE TRULY KEEP GOING LIKE THIS WITHOUT MEAT AND DRINK?
"THE GREAT ALL THAT IS" HAS EVERYTHING THAT MAKES UP LIFE.
ALL AROUND US ARE MORSELS MUCH TOO TINY TO SEE. MY MOTHER TIMMAIN TAUGHT ME HOW TO GATHER THEM INTO OURSELVES, TO NOURISH US.
SO THAT'S WHY WE'RE NOT HUNGRY OR THIRSTY!
THE GO-BACK IN ME SAYS PUCKERNUTS! BUT THE SKYWISE PART ALMOST UNDERSTANDS.
BUT I LOVE FOOD! LOVE TO SMELL AND CHOMP AND MUNCH IT!
WE'LL TRY TO MAKE THIS JOURNEY SHORT, TRINKET.
BUT HOW DO E FIND FATHER IN ALL OF THAT?
THE LOSS OF CUTTER SENT SKYWISE OUT THERE, SEEKING.
MAYBE...
♫ FROM STAR TO STAR WE TRAVELED FAR--FALLING, THEN, FROM BLIND PRIDE'S SCAR--OUR YEARNING FOR LEARNING--BROUGHT US WHERE WE ARE. ♪
♪ THE QUEST UNWOUND--THE TRUTH WE FOUND--LEFT US WITH A CHOICE PROFOUND: ONCE MORE ROAM THE STARHOME--OR CLING TO THIS GROUND.

LEETAH'S LULLABY! CUTTER LOVED HER TO SING IT.
SOMETIMES, SHE SAID, IT BRINGS HIM TO HER!
♪PERHAPS NOT AS INTENDED--BROKEN WHEELS GET MENDED--AND BROKEN HEARTS HEAL LARGER-- FOR THE BREAKING.♬
♫LOVING IS ALWAYS-- AND LIVING IS ALWAYS--EACH FEARLESS BREATH WE TAKE-- IS WORTH THE TAKING.♩
YES... YES! THE SONG OF "ALWAYS."
GASP!
WHAT? WHAT?!
FOLLOW HIS HUM!
CUTTER'S SPIRIT...
IT'S GONE!

I DO SENSE IT!
OH NO...
A CALL FROM FAAAAAAATHER!
WAAAAAAA
AAAAHHHHHHH!

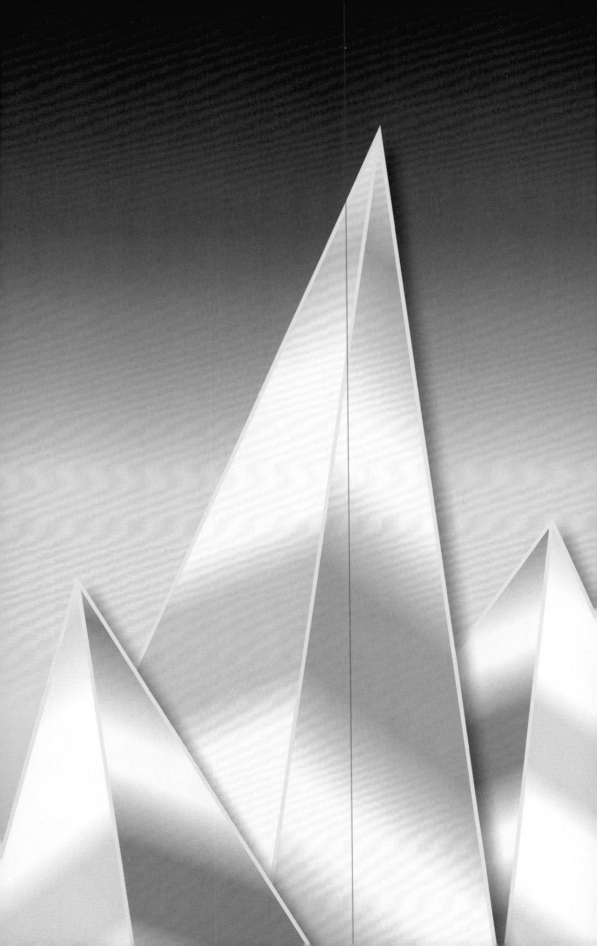

POST-CATACLYSMIC HUMANS, REDUCED TO A STARK EXISTENCE OF BARE SURVIVAL, SCAVENGE ABOUT THE BLASTED HUSK OF THE SCULPERS' LONG-DORMANT STAR VESSEL--
--ATTRACTED BY SKYWISE'S RADIANT "CANDLE."
SO BRIGHT! REMINDS ME OF--OF SOMETHING BETTER! SOMETHING LOST!
IT'S SOME KIND OF TREASURE! WE'LL HAVE IT!
LOOK! A MISSILE!
WHOOOOSH
NO! NO EXPLOSION!
SOME SORT OF TRANSPORT, THEN! IT'S LANDING!
GLOWS LIKE OUR TREASURE! WE'LL HAVE THEM BOTH!

FROM THE NEWLY SETTLED POD, ITS LUSTER OBSCURED BY NOXIOUS CLOUDS--

--THREE GASPING FIGURES EMERGE.

≈COUGH COUGH≈

≈GASP!≈ WHAT A **STENCH!** IT **BURNS** INSIDE MY CHEST!

≈COUGH HACK≈

AND BELOW, IN A CLUTTERED LIBRARY IN THE **SCULPERS'** REALM...

OOOOO-OOOOO! **BIG STARHOME** HUM!

COMES **NEW!** COMES **NOW!**

CAN IT BE, HIGH ONE **SKYWISE,** THAT YOUR CANDLE HAS LURED IN ANOTHER VESSEL SO SOON?

IS POD-POD! **THISTLECAP** KNOWS! GO SEE! GO SEE!

AND...

≈WHEEZE≈ WE **MUST** GO BACK INSIDE!

CAN'T ≈GAG!≈ CAN'T **BREATHE!**

OH HORRORS!

WE'RE GOING TO **DIE** IN THIS AWFUL PLACE!

PANICKING, THE PAMPERED TROLL PRINCESS HEEDLESSLY DASHES...AWAY FROM SAFETY!

NO! NO! I'M SLIPPING!
EEEYAAAH! THEY'LL EAT ME!
ALIENS! INVADERS!
TRINKET!
POP
THINKING QUICKLY, SKYWISE'S YOUNGEST "JINKS" FROM HER SISTER'S SIDE--
UUFF!
WHISSH
POP
--AND INSTANTLY SCOOPS UP HER FLAILING FRIEND!
AAAAAH!
COUGH COUGH
QUICK! INTO THE POD!
no no no!
HIGHTHINGS AND GIRL DIG-DIG HERE! DOWN-DOWN! SLIDE DOWN!
ASTONISHED TO SEE HER CHILDHOOD PRESERVER COMPANION--

--JINK OBEYS AND FLOATS DOWN, INTO THE DERELICT SHIP--
--WHILE YUN FINDS HER OWN WAY IN.
HELLO! HELLO!
SPIRES OF PALACE CITY!
GASP! MORE HIGH ONES HAVE COME?!
WE NEVER DARED HOPE FOR SUCH JOYOUS TIMES!
THISTLECAP KNOWS FANCY DIG-DIG-GIRL...
...KNOWS GROWLER-RIDER GIRL...BUT OTHER?!
YUN!
WHAT IN THE NAMES OF THE TEN CHIEFS ARE YOU DOING HERE?
SEARCHING FOR YOU, FATHER!
MADE A GOOD JOB OF IT, TOO, DIDN'T WE?

ELL, NOW! HAT'S THIS HARMING AGGAGE OU CARRY, EAUTIFUL IGH ONE?
ALLOW US, DAINTY MAIDEN!
CLEARLY SHE'S A DISTANT COUSIN!
HMMM... FOREIGN-LOOKING, BUT FETCHING!
PERHAPS. WHERE YOU ARE FROM? YOU ARE SOMEONE SPECIAL?
GIGGLE GIGGLE AM I DREAMING?! I MUST BE!
YUN...
I-I CAN'T BELIEVE THIS!
BUT... WHO'S THAT WITH YOU?
OH, FOR FREEFOOT'S SAKE!
DON'T YOU KNOW MY "HUM"--
--FATHER?!
GASP!
JINK! MY LITTLE CUB! CHOKE OH, STARS!
HAS IT TRULY BEEN SO LONG?

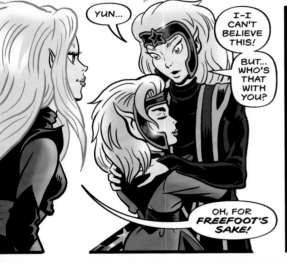

YOU'RE ALL GROWN UP! I *DID* ABANDON YOU! HOW COULD I? WHY?! I *PROMISED!*
HOW DO I SAY I'M SORRY?!
MY SWEET SIRE, YOU COULDN'T HAVE DONE ANYTHING ELSE.
YOU *MEAN*...SKYWISE *ALWAYS* DESERTS HIS CLOSEST ONES?
NO...*NO!* I HAVE COME TO SET THINGS RIGHT!
IT SEEMS THERE ARE STORIES TO BE TOLD--
--AND MYSTERIES TO BE SOLVED. DO COME BELOW--
--AND LET US WELCOME YOU PROPERLY!
THANK YOU, SCULPERS.
SHORTLY...
SO YOU ARE A *"TROLL"!* HIGH ONE SKYWISE TAUGHT US THAT INTERESTING NAME.
AND YOUR TITLE IS... HOW DO YOU SAY IT?
*PRIN...CESS!* SHE SAID *"PRINCESS"!*
DOES THAT MEAN YOU ARE A POET? A MAKER? A LEADER? A TEACHER?
WELL, ON MY WORLD A PRINCESS ISN'T ASKED TO DO MUCH OF *ANYTHING,* REALLY.

LEFT TO THEMSELVES BY THEIR DISCREET HOSTS, SKYWISE AND JINK RENEW THEIR BOND--
--WITH AN ACHING MIX OF JOY AND REGRET.
YOU'RE AS PERFECT AS TIMMAIN!
I SEE ME--AND EVEN MORE OF HER--IN YOU!
FORGIVE ME, IF YOU CAN!
I SHOULD ASK THAT OF YOU. A CHILDISH MISTAKE I MADE--
--CAUSED YOU MORE ANGUISH THAN THE PAIN I TRIED TO STOP.
PAIN?
BECAUSE HIS DEATH HURT YOU SO...
DEATH?!
WHOSE DEATH?
I TOUCHED YOU LIKE THIS--
--AND TOOK FROM YOU ALL REMEMBRANCE--
--OF ONE WHO KNEW YOUR SOUL NAME...AND YOU HIS.
I TOOK HIM FROM YOUR MIND...BUT NOT FROM YOUR HEART.
SO YOU LEFT--TO SEEK, AMONG THE STARS--
--THE NAMELESS THING YOU KNEW WAS MISSING.
YOU DIDN'T DESERT MOTHER AND ME.
NEITHER SHE NOR I HAVE EVER FELT THAT WAY.
"HIS DEATH...?" I-I DON'T... WHO DO YOU MEAN?
I CAME TO TAKE YOU BACK TO THE BEST, THE ONLY PLACE--

"--WHERE THAT QUESTION CAN BE ANSWERED! BACK TO THE WORLD OF TWO MOONS!"
ARCHEOLOGIST PAR TOLFSSON CAN HARDLY BELIEVE HIS GOOD FORTUNE. SOMEHOW, HE HAS GAINED THE EAR OF THE UNITED INSECT CLANS' HEAD COUNCILWOMAN.
AS SHE GUIDES HIM NEARER THE FATHER TREE, HE SELECTS CAREFULLY FROM THE THOUSAND QUESTIONS PRESSING HIS EAGER TONGUE.
FOR HE KNOWS ZAZAPAT IKOPEK IS ONE WHOSE TRUST, ONCE ABUSED, CAN NEVER BE REGAINED.
WOULD YOU TELL ME ABOUT YOUR ANCESTRESS SHUNA? IT'S SAID SHE WAS MUCH MORE THAN A SAGE AND TEACHER.
MMPH...
MORE THAN ANY HUMAN PERSON WHO EVER WALKED THIS LAND.
THE GOOD SPIRITS MADE HER SO. I DON'T CARE IF YOU BELIEVE SHE LIVED SEVERAL HUNDRED YEARS OR NOT. SHE DID.
SHE COULD TALK WITH HER MIND. AND SHE FOUND OTHERS WHOSE MINDS SHE COULD SEE INTO.
THOSE WHO HAD...UH--
PSYCHIC POTENTIAL!
SHE TRAINED SOME OF YOUR LONG-AGO TRIBESFOLK AND THEN--

AND THEN, MUCH LATER, ANYONE WHO HAD SIGNS OF THE GIFT. YEAH.
SHE WAS GENEROUS TO ALL WHO WANTED TO LEARN. BUT ONLY A VERY FEW EVER REALLY COULD.
SHE TAUGHT AT THE RUINS OF BLUE MOUNTAIN?
THE SACRED RUINS. SHE WAS A SACRED BEING!
SHE COULD TAP INTO THE MAGICAL ENERGIES OF THE PLACE.
MAY I ASK WHAT HAPPENED TO HER?
SHE JUST PLAIN GOT TIRED, GRUB...TIRED OF LIVING FOREVER.
I DON'T BLAME HER.
ONE DAY SHE UP AND ASKED THE GOOD SPIRITS TO MAKE HER MORTAL AGAIN. FINISHED OUT A NORMAL OLD AGE. DIED SOME HUNDRED YEARS AGO.
HER STUDENTS, THOUGH, THEY CARRIED ON HER TEACHINGS ALMOST LIKE A RELIGION--
--'TIL IT TURNED INTO SELF-WORSHIP. THEY GAVE IN TO THEIR UGLIEST URGES--
--AND DAMN NEAR KILLED EACH OTHER OFF.

SO HAVE YOU DONE ENOUGH DIGGING ON YOUR OWN TO KNOW WHAT HAPPENED NEXT?
THE LEGEND OF BLUE MOUNTAIN...THE DEEP, DARK FORCES THERE, LEFT BEHIND BY AN EVIL, DEMONIC SPIRIT.
ALL THAT FEUDING STIRRED THE BAD MAGIC UP AGAIN...SO THE STORY GOES.
BUT WHAT FINALLY STOPPED IT? WHAT DROVE THE DISCIPLES AWAY FROM BLUE MOUNTAIN'S REMAINS--
--SO THAT, TODAY, THEY MUST USE MACHINES TO AUGMENT THEIR POWERS?
"A CARETAKER..." QUEEN BEE MUTTERS, "...ONE WHO'D BEEN THERE IN THE DISTANT BEFORE-TIME. HE CAME BACK FROM THE STARS--
"--BURROWED DEEP BENEATH THE RUBBLE. HE BALANCES THE LIGHT AND DARK ENERGIES EMBEDDED IN THE ANCIENT STONE."
SO THE STORY GOES.
QUEEN BEE! PLEASE! TELL ME!
IS IT AN ELF?
COME ON, GRUB. THE GOOD SPIRITS AR EVERYWHER JUST ACCEPT IT--

"--AND DON'T GET SO ALL-FIRED WORKED UP ABOUT *NAMES.*"
THERE IS ONLY ONE PLACE YOU SHOULD BE WHEN YOU *REMEMBER*--
--INSIDE THE *FATHER TREE!*
MAYBE YOU'LL BE SAD AGAIN.
BUT BETTER THAT, THAN ALL YOU'VE BEEN THROUGH--
--WANDERING AIMLESSLY, NEVER KNOWING HOW TO COMPLETE YOUR QUEST.
BUT-BUT SHE-CUBS...
YOUR POD AND MINE, COMBINED, PROBABLY HAVE POWER ENOUGH TO *RESTORE* THE MELTED STAR VESSEL ABOVE, AND--
SKYWISE...
YOU'RE RIGHT. I *MUST* FACE--
--WHATEVER'S COMING TO ME.
YOU GOT SOMETHING TO *DO* FOR YOURSELF, GO DO IT!
YOU CAN *ALWAYS* RETURN!
YES. FOR US, THERE *IS* TIME ENOUGH--
--FOR *ANYTHING!*
BESIDES, WE CAN LEAVE ANOTHER "CANDLE" TO SEND OUT A CALL.

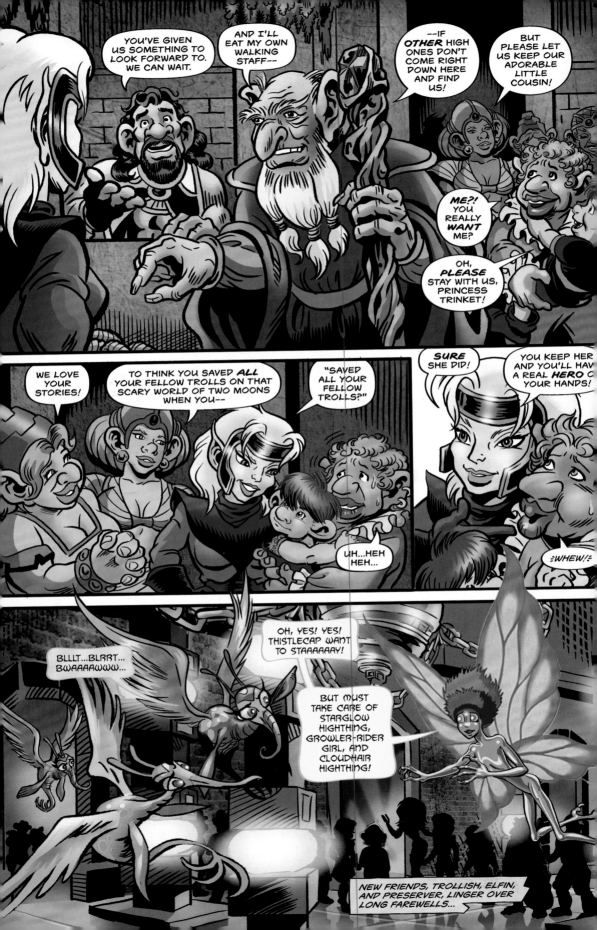

YOU'VE GIVEN US SOMETHING TO LOOK FORWARD TO. WE CAN WAIT.

AND I'LL EAT MY OWN WALKING STAFF--

--IF *OTHER* HIGH ONES DON'T COME RIGHT DOWN HERE AND FIND US!

BUT PLEASE LET US KEEP OUR ADORABLE LITTLE COUSIN!

*ME?!* YOU REALLY *WANT* ME?

OH, *PLEASE* STAY WITH US, PRINCESS TRINKET!

WE LOVE YOUR STORIES!

TO THINK YOU SAVED *ALL* YOUR FELLOW TROLLS ON THAT SCARY WORLD OF TWO MOONS WHEN YOU--

"SAVED ALL YOUR FELLOW TROLLS?"

*SURE* SHE DID!

YOU KEEP HER AND YOU'LL HAV A REAL *HERO* O YOUR HANDS!

UH...HEH HEH...

≡WHEW!≡

BLLLT...BLRRT... BWAAAAWWW...

OH, YES! YES! THISTLECAP WANT TO STAAAAAAY!

BUT MUST TAKE CARE OF STARGLOW HIGHTHING, GROWLER-RIDER GIRL, AND CLOUDHAIR HIGHTHING!

NEW FRIENDS, TROLLISH, ELFIN, AND PRESERVER, LINGER OVER LONG FAREWELLS...

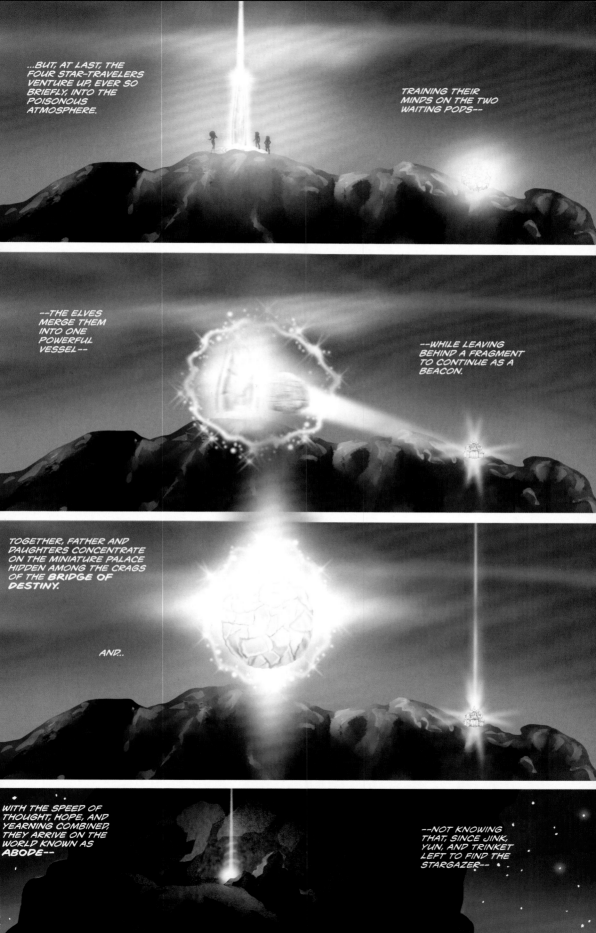

...BUT, AT LAST, THE FOUR STAR-TRAVELERS VENTURE UP, EVER SO BRIEFLY, INTO THE POISONOUS ATMOSPHERE.

TRAINING THEIR MINDS ON THE TWO WAITING PODS--

--THE ELVES MERGE THEM INTO ONE POWERFUL VESSEL--

--WHILE LEAVING BEHIND A FRAGMENT TO CONTINUE AS A BEACON.

TOGETHER, FATHER AND DAUGHTERS CONCENTRATE ON THE MINIATURE PALACE HIDDEN AMONG THE CRAGS OF THE **BRIDGE OF DESTINY.**

AND...

WITH THE SPEED OF THOUGHT, HOPE, AND YEARNING COMBINED, THEY ARRIVE ON THE WORLD KNOWN AS **ABODE**--

--NOT KNOWING THAT, SINCE JINK, YUN, AND TRINKET LEFT TO FIND THE STARGAZER--

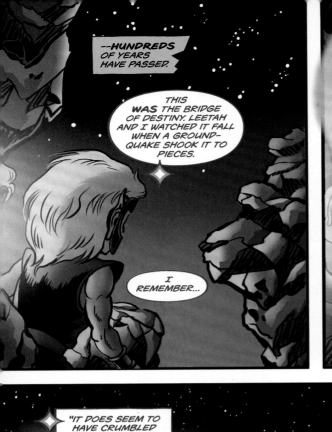

--HUNDREDS OF YEARS HAVE PASSED.

THIS **WAS** THE BRIDGE OF DESTINY. LEETAH AND I WATCHED IT FALL WHEN A GROUND-QUAKE SHOOK IT TO PIECES.

I REMEMBER...

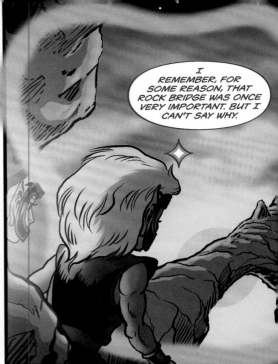

I REMEMBER, FOR SOME REASON, THAT ROCK BRIDGE WAS ONCE VERY IMPORTANT. BUT I CAN'T SAY WHY.

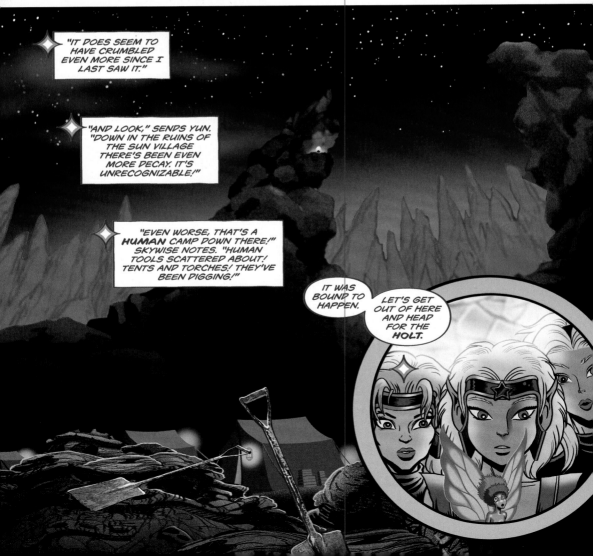

"IT DOES SEEM TO HAVE CRUMBLED EVEN MORE SINCE I LAST SAW IT."

"AND LOOK," SENDS YUN. "DOWN IN THE RUINS OF THE SUN VILLAGE THERE'S BEEN EVEN MORE DECAY. IT'S UNRECOGNIZABLE!"

"EVEN WORSE, THAT'S A **HUMAN** CAMP DOWN THERE!" SKYWISE NOTES. "HUMAN TOOLS SCATTERED ABOUT! TENTS AND TORCHES! THEY'VE BEEN DIGGING!"

IT WAS BOUND TO HAPPEN.

LET'S GET OUT OF HERE AND HEAD FOR THE **HOLT**.

LET ME DO IT, SHE-CUBS! WHATEVER ELSE I'VE FORGOTTEN--
WHEEEEEE-EEEE!
WHIIISSSHHHHHH
"--I DO KNOW HOW TO GET US TO THE FATHER TREE!"
AT THE SAME TIME...
THIS IS AS FAR AS I CAN TAKE YOU, GRUB. IF YOU WANT--
--GO SEE WHAT YOU CAN SEE FROM THAT SMALL RISE AHEAD.
!!!
HOLY, HALLOWED SISTER-BROTHER OF--

A WAVE OF THE HAND MAKES THE INTERIOR OF THE HOVERING POD TRANSPARENT AND..
:GASP!: THE HOLT! SO STRANGE TO SEE IT AGAIN!
WAIT! SOMETHING'S OFF!
IT'S NIGHT, BUT THERE'S NO MOVEMENT! NO SIGN, EVEN, OF THE WOLVES.
SHOULD WE GET OUT AND INVESTIGATE?
MIGHT NOT BE SAFE.
YUN SENDS...
AND..
NO ANSWER. I DON'T LIKE IT!
WHERE ARE THE WOLF-RIDERS?
I KNOW! WHERE GOLDRUFF IS, THE WOLFRIDERS WILL BE.
IF HE STILL WEARS MY GIFT...
A MOMENT LATER...
:CHUCKLE:
HOLY CRAP...HOLY CRAP...HOLY CRAP...
WHEN WAS THE LAST TIME YOU SAW A FALLING STAR STOP, HOVER, THEN FALL UP AGAIN, GRUB?
LOOKS LIKE YOU WERE MEANT TO BE HERE.

AND, FAR FROM FATHER TREE HOLT, IN A RUGGED WILDERNESS...
CAW! CAW! CAW!
WELL, WELL! BENT BEAK'S BACK!
AND NOT A WORM TO SHOW FOR IT!
IF YOU'RE HERE TO BEG SCRAPS FROM US, TANGLE-FEATHERS, YOU'LL HAVE TO STAND BEHIND BLACKWING.
SHE GETS FIRST CHEW!
CAW!
CAW!
THINK YELLING'LL GET YOU YOUR WAY, YOU FOOLISH--
GASP!
HEY, SHAGBACK MEAT! WHAT'S THAT?!
HUNH! HAVEN'T SEEN ONE OF THOSE IN MORE EIGHTS THAN I CAN TELL!

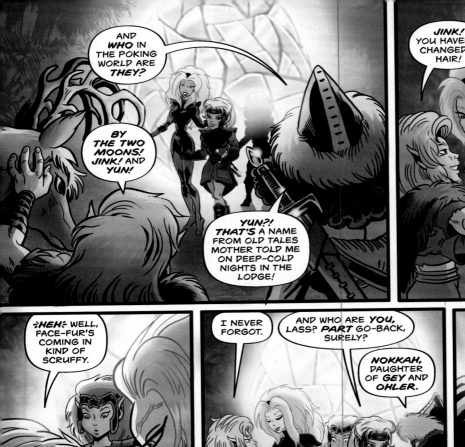

AND **WHO** IN THE POKING WORLD ARE **THEY?**

BY **THE TWO MOONS! JINK!** AND **YUN!**

**YUN?!** THAT'S A NAME FROM **OLD** TALES MOTHER TOLD ME ON **DEEP-COLD** NIGHTS IN THE **LODGE!**

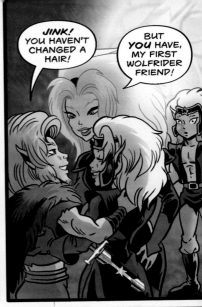

**JINK!** YOU HAVEN'T CHANGED A **HAIR!**

BUT **YOU** HAVE, MY **FIRST** WOLFRIDER FRIEND!

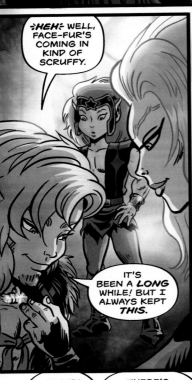

=HEH= WELL, FACE-FUR'S COMING IN KIND OF SCRUFFY.

IT'S BEEN A **LONG** WHILE! BUT I ALWAYS KEPT **THIS.**

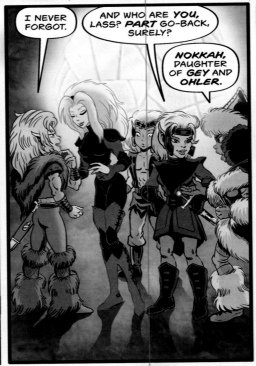

I NEVER FORGOT.

AND WHO ARE **YOU,** LASS? **PART** GO-BACK, SURELY?

**NOKKAH,** DAUGHTER OF **GEY** AND **OHLER.**

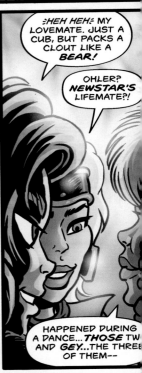

=HEH HEH= MY LOVEMATE. JUST A **CUB,** BUT PACKS A CLOUT LIKE A **BEAR!**

**OHLER? NEWSTAR'S** LIFEMATE?!

HAPPENED DURING A DANCE... **THOSE** TW AND **GEY...** THE THREE OF THEM--

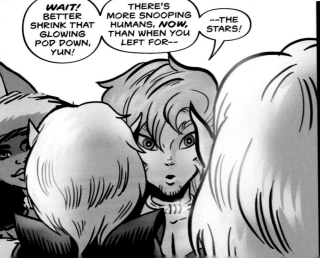

**WAIT!** BETTER SHRINK THAT GLOWING POD DOWN, **YUN!**

THERE'S MORE SNOOPING HUMANS, **NOW,** THAN WHEN YOU LEFT FOR--

--THE **STARS!**

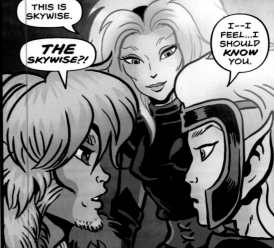

THIS IS SKYWISE.

**THE** SKYWISE?!

I--I FEEL...I SHOULD **KNOW** YOU.

GOLDRUFF, SON OF LEETAH AND CUTTER.
CUTTER...?
HE DOES NOT YET REMEMBER.
BUT LEETAH, EMBER, CLEARBROOK, AND PIKE--
WHERE'S THE REST OF THE TRIBE?
BACK THAT WAY, TWO DAYS' RIDE TOWARD "SUN-GOES-UP."
EXCEPT FOR REDLANCE AND NIGHTFALL. THEY'RE SEEING IN THE ROOTLESS ONES' DELL, NOW.
BUT WHY?
WHY DID THE WOLFRIDERS LEAVE THE HOLT?
THE WOLFRIDERS AND GO-BACKS BLENDED INTO ONE TRIBE, Y'KNOW.
TEIR TAUGHT THE GO-BACKS NOT TO PEN THEIR DEER, BUT TO LET THEM ROAM FREE--
--AND HOW TO CALL THEIR MOUNTS, AS WE DO OUR WOLVES.
"THE HUMAN INSECT TRIBES BECAME POWERFUL ALLIES.
"THEY KEPT THEIR PROMISE TO US--
"--AND MADE THE LAND ALL AROUND FATHER TREE HOLT, FAR AS THE EYE COULD SEE, FORBIDDEN TO TRESPASSERS.

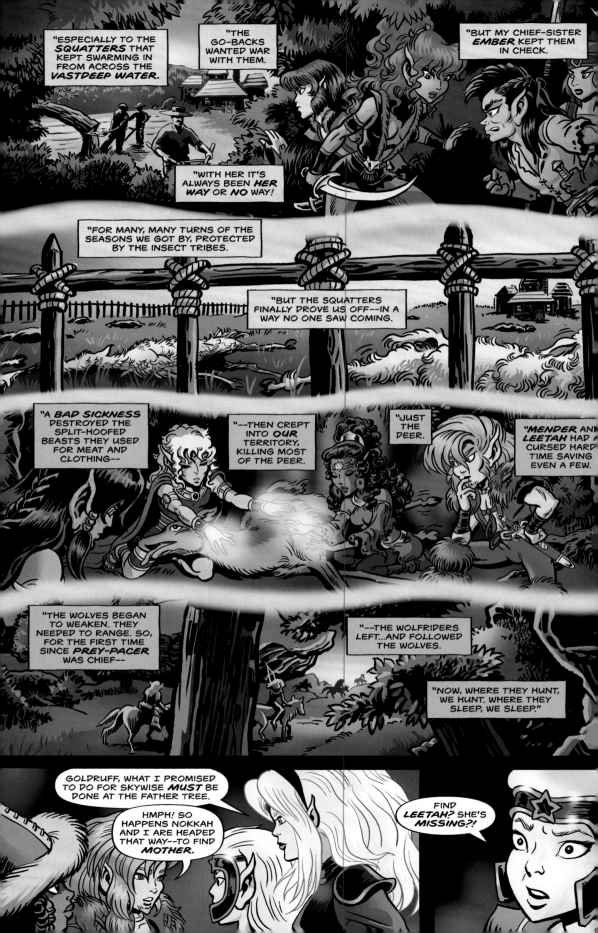

"ESPECIALLY TO THE **SQUATTERS** THAT KEPT SWARMING IN FROM ACROSS THE **VASTDEEP WATER.**

"THE GO-BACKS WANTED WAR WITH THEM.

"BUT MY CHIEF-SISTER **EMBER** KEPT THEM IN CHECK.

"WITH HER IT'S ALWAYS BEEN **HER WAY** OR **NO** WAY!

"FOR MANY, MANY TURNS OF THE SEASONS WE GOT BY, PROTECTED BY THE INSECT TRIBES.

"BUT THE SQUATTERS FINALLY DROVE US OFF--IN A WAY NO ONE SAW COMING.

"A **BAD SICKNESS** DESTROYED THE SPLIT-HOOFED BEASTS THEY USED FOR MEAT AND CLOTHING--

"--THEN CREPT INTO **OUR** TERRITORY, KILLING MOST OF THE DEER.

"JUST THE DEER.

"**MENDER** AND **LEETAH** HAD A CURSED HARD TIME SAVING EVEN A FEW.

"THE WOLVES BEGAN TO WEAKEN. THEY NEEDED TO RANGE. SO, FOR THE FIRST TIME SINCE **PREY-PACER** WAS CHIEF--

"--THE WOLFRIDERS LEFT...AND FOLLOWED THE WOLVES.

"NOW, WHERE THEY HUNT, WE HUNT. WHERE THEY SLEEP, WE SLEEP."

GOLDRUFF, WHAT I PROMISED TO DO FOR SKYWISE **MUST** BE DONE AT THE FATHER TREE.

HMPH! SO HAPPENS NOKKAH AND I ARE HEADED THAT WAY--TO FIND **MOTHER.**

FIND **LEETAH?** SHE'S **MISSING?!**

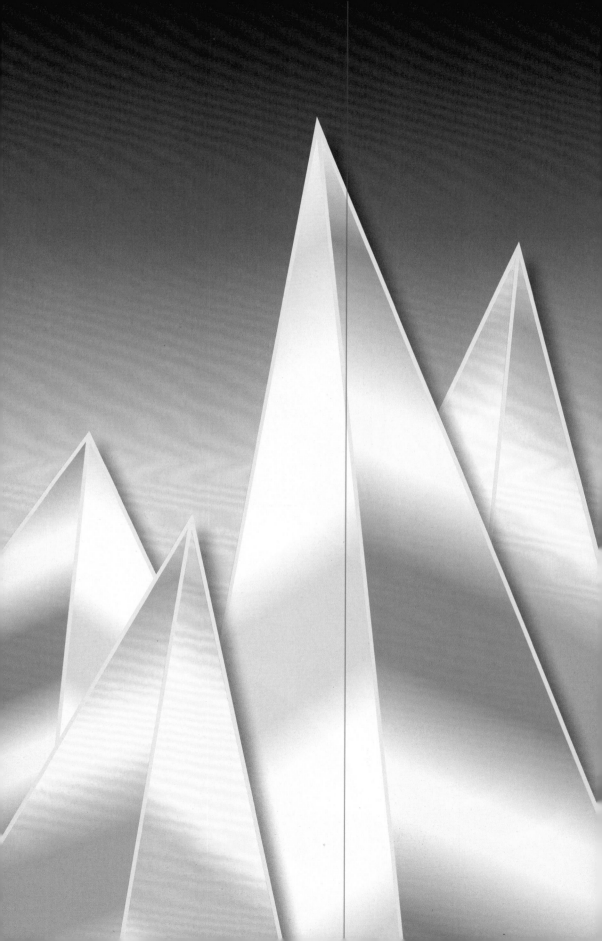

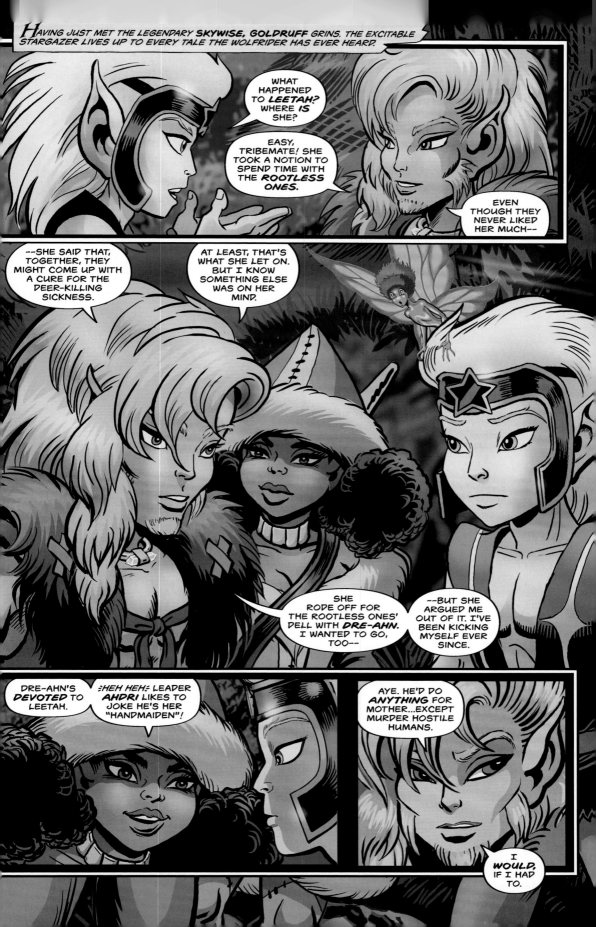

HAVING JUST MET THE LEGENDARY **SKYWISE**, **GOLDRUFF** GRINS. THE EXCITABLE STARGAZER LIVES UP TO EVERY TALE THE WOLFRIDER HAS EVER HEARD.

WHAT HAPPENED TO **LEETAH?** WHERE **IS** SHE?

EASY, TRIBEMATE! SHE TOOK A NOTION TO SPEND TIME WITH THE **ROOTLESS ONES.**

EVEN THOUGH THEY NEVER LIKED HER MUCH--

--SHE SAID THAT, TOGETHER, THEY MIGHT COME UP WITH A CURE FOR THE DEER-KILLING SICKNESS.

AT LEAST, THAT'S WHAT SHE LET ON. BUT I KNOW SOMETHING ELSE WAS ON HER MIND.

SHE RODE OFF FOR THE ROOTLESS ONES' DELL WITH **DRE-AHN.** I WANTED TO GO, TOO--

--BUT SHE ARGUED ME OUT OF IT. I'VE BEEN KICKING MYSELF EVER SINCE.

DRE-AHN'S **DEVOTED** TO LEETAH.

⸬HEH HEH⸬ LEADER **AHDRI** LIKES TO JOKE HE'S HER "HANDMAIDEN"!

AYE. HE'D DO **ANYTHING** FOR MOTHER...EXCEPT MURDER HOSTILE HUMANS.

I **WOULD,** IF I HAD TO.

WE'VE BEEN TRACKING DRE-AHN'S PONY. BUT WE'RE STILL DAYS BEHIND THEM-- EH?!
DOES LEETAH HAVE A CRYSTAL LIKE THIS ONE, MY FRIEND IN THE FURS?
HMPH!
SURE! MOST WOLFRIDERS DO. THEY WERE GIFTS TO REMEMBER THE PALACE DWELLERS BY--
--GIVEN TO US BY THE GREAT TANNER MOONSHADE.
MOONSHADE...
WELL, THEN LEETAH'S CRYSTAL WILL GUIDE US TO HER AS EASILY AS WE FOUND YOU.
GULP BEEN A LONG...LONG TIME SINCE I DID THAT KIND OF TRAVEL.
HUNH! YOU CAN HAVE IT!
YOU'RE NOT GETTING ME INSIDE A THING THAT STRETCHES AND SQUASHES AND FLIES AROUND LIKE THAT!
HERE, KEEP IT SO I CAN FIND YOU AGAIN. IF I CAN SEE MOTHER SAFELY TO THE ROOTLESS ONES' DELL--
--I'LL COME BACK TO YOU WITHOUT A CARE.
WAIT FOR ME HERE?
I'LL WAIT.
BLACKWING LIKES ME BETTER'N YOU, ANYWAY.
SMAC

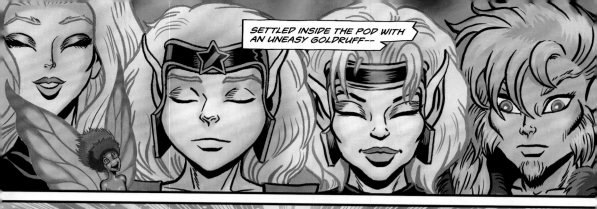

SETTLED INSIDE THE POD WITH AN UNEASY GOLDRUFF--

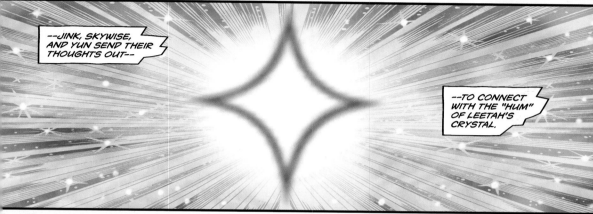

--JINK, SKYWISE, AND YUN SEND THEIR THOUGHTS OUT--

--TO CONNECT WITH THE "HUM" OF LEETAH'S CRYSTAL.

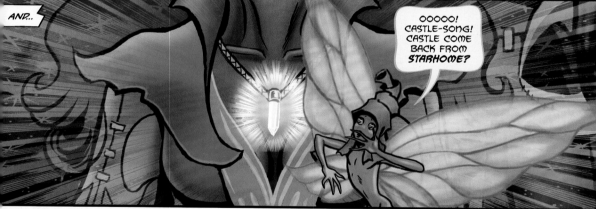

AND...

OOOOO! CASTLE-SONG! CASTLE COME BACK FROM STARHOME?

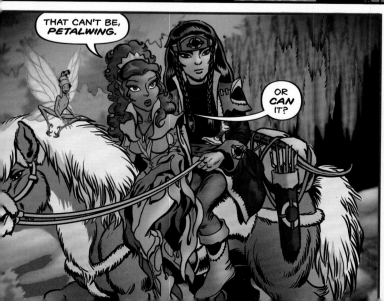

THAT CAN'T BE, PETALWING.

OR CAN IT?

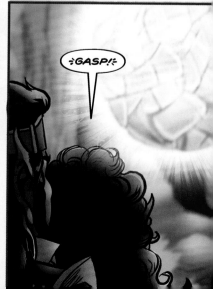

÷GASP!÷

AND EVEN BEFORE THE POD HAS SETTLED TO THE GROUND...
LEETAH!
THISTLECAP!
SKYWISE?! OH, SKYWISE
PETALWING!
BREEE-DEET
DEEDLE-DEE-DEE
SOON, WHEN TEARS OF HEARTFELT REUNION ARE DRY AND OPEN-SENT EXPLANATIONS GIVEN...
YES, THE FATHER TREE!
FOR THIS GREATEST OF HEALINGS, YOU MUST GO THERE.
PLEASE COME WITH US, MOTHER OF MEMORY. I SEE HOW FATHER'S EYES GLOW AT YOUR NEARNESS.
WHEN HE'S ABLE TO RECALL EVERY LOST MOMENT, YOUR ARMS WILL SURELY BE THE FIRST HE SEEKS.
OF COURSE! I--
OH!

WE MUST DELAY OUR JOURNEY TO THE LAND OF THE ROOTLESS ONES.
FIRST, WE MUST GO TO FATHER TREE HOLT.
THE ENIGMATIC ELFIN SINGER SIMPLY LOOKS AT HER AND STROKES HIS PONY'S RAGGED MANE.
OH, HIS NO-HUMP! JINK...YUN... CAN YOU...?
EASILY!
DONE AND DONE, MOTHER OF MEMORY!
WHOOOSH
WHOOOSH

EVEN AS THE TWIN PODS STREAK TOWARD THE HOLT, ZAZAPAT IKOPEK, KNOWN TO THE WORLD AS "QUEEN BEE," ADMONISHES...
TIME TO GO, GRUB. YOU'VE SEEN ENOUGH.
WAIT! THE TREE! DOES IT HAVE A NAME?
NOT FOR YOUR EARS.
WHA--?! NOW WHAT'S HAPPENING?!
RUM-TATA-TUM TUM TUM RUM-TATA-TUM TUM TUM
HEAR THE DRUMS? THERE HASN'T BEEN A NIGHT LIKE THIS--
--OF STARS COMING AND GOING--SINCE THE GOOD SPIRITS' CHIEF OF CHIEFS DIED.
"CHIEF OF CHIEFS"?
FROM OUR DEEP LORE.
FOSTER FATHER TO MY ANCESTRESS SHUNA. IT'S SAID HE CAME CLOSE TO BEING HUMAN HIMSELF, SO HE WAS ABLE--
--TO FORGE BONDS OF LOVE AND TRUST BETWEEN HIS SPIRIT FOLK AND THE INSECT TRIBES.
HEY! GET THAT HUNGRY GLEAM OUT OF YOUR EYE!
YOU GO CRAZY AND FLIT ON ME--
--AND I'LL HAVE TO STOP YOU.
I'D KILL MYSELF RATHER THAN BETRAY ANYTHING I LEARN HERE. BELIEVE THAT!
BUT I WILL DIE--FROM NEEDING TO KNOW--

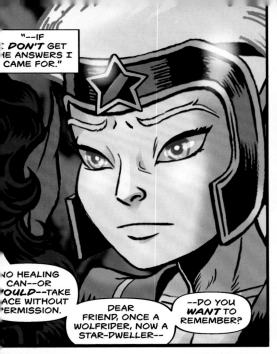

"--IF I *DON'T* GET THE ANSWERS I CAME FOR."

NO HEALING CAN--OR *WOULD*--TAKE PLACE WITHOUT PERMISSION.

DEAR FRIEND, ONCE A WOLFRIDER, NOW A STAR-DWELLER--

--DO YOU *WANT* TO REMEMBER?

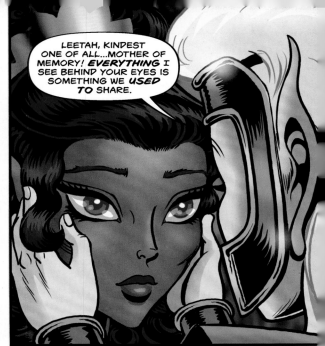

LEETAH, KINDEST ONE OF ALL...MOTHER OF MEMORY! *EVERYTHING* I SEE BEHIND YOUR EYES IS SOMETHING WE *USED TO* SHARE.

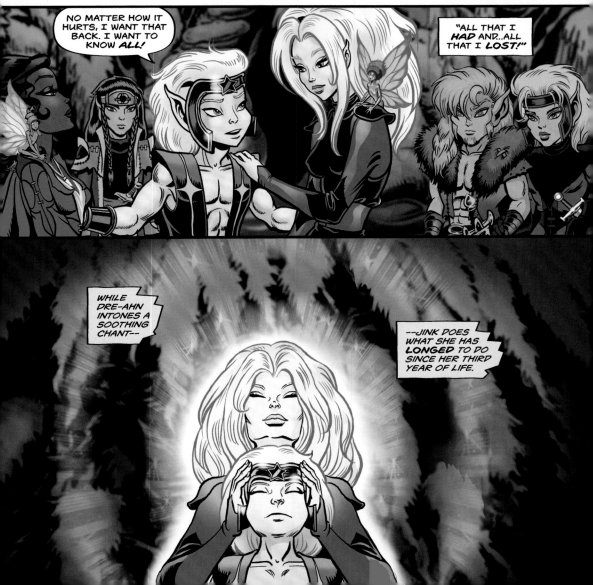

NO MATTER HOW IT HURTS, I WANT THAT BACK. I WANT TO KNOW *ALL!*

"ALL THAT I *HAD* AND...ALL THAT I *LOST!*"

WHILE DRE-AHN INTONES A SOOTHING CHANT--

--JINK DOES WHAT SHE HAS *LONGED* TO DO SINCE HER THIRD YEAR OF LIFE.

TAM...
...BELOVED BROTHER...
...KEEPER OF MY SOUL NAME...
...FRIEND OF MY BODY...
...AND SPIRIT...
...TIED BEYOND ALL UNTYING...
...FOREVER!

OH, TAM... TAM!
I REMEMBER EVERYTHING ABOUT US!
THE FATHER TREE...CUTTER SWORE ON HIS HEART IT WOULD ALWAYS STAND!
HE'S HERE. I KNOW IT!
GO.
AFTER MORE THAN FIVE HUNDRED TURNS OF THE SEASONS, SKYWISE ONCE AGAIN ENTERS THE FATHER TREE.
HE CLIMBS UP--
--ALL THE WAY UP--
--INTO THE HOLLOWS OF THE HIGHEST BRANCH--
--WHERE HE CAN GO NO FARTHER.

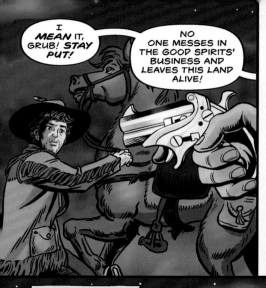

I **MEAN** IT, GRUB! **STAY PUT!**

NO ONE MESSES IN THE GOOD SPIRITS' BUSINESS AND LEAVES THIS LAND ALIVE!

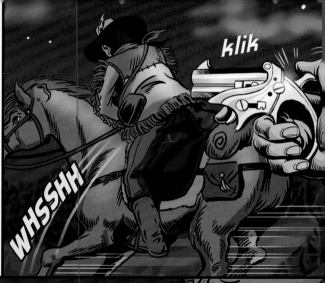

**klik**

WHSSHH

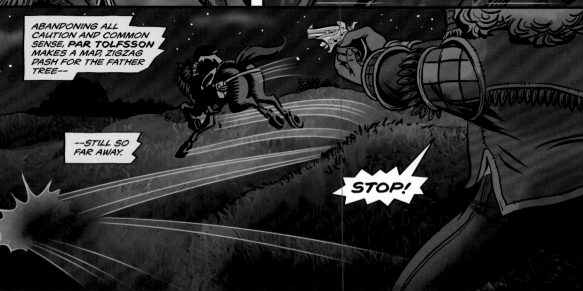

ABANDONING ALL CAUTION AND COMMON SENSE, **PAR TOLFSSON** MAKES A MAD, ZIGZAG DASH FOR THE FATHER TREE--

--STILL SO FAR AWAY.

STOP!

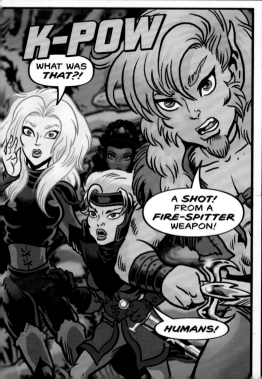

**K-POW**

WHAT WAS **THAT**?!

A **SHOT!** FROM A **FIRE-SPITTER** WEAPON!

HUMANS!

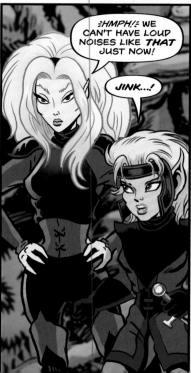

≡HMPH!≡ WE CAN'T HAVE LOUD NOISES LIKE **THAT** JUST NOW!

JINK...!

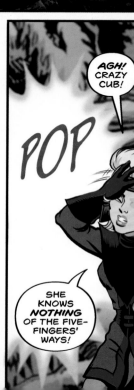

**POP**

AGH! CRAZY CUB!

SHE KNOWS **NOTHING** OF THE FIVE-FINGERS' WAYS!

POP
HUH?!
POP
POP
WHO?!
WHA--?!
POP
STOP! HOLD STILL!
WHAT ARE YOU?!
POP
THE PULL OF THIS WORLD--TIRING ME OUT!
BUT I MUST LURE HIM **FAR** FROM THE HOLT!
NOTHING MUST DISTURB--

"--FATHER'S HEALING!"
TAM... IT'S ME. IT'S FAHR!
I GAVE UP MY WOLF BLOOD... REMEMBER?
I'M A HIGH ONE NOW!
BUT THIS WORLD'S SCENT IS STILL ON ME.
OUR ROOTS, YOURS AND MINE, GO AS DEEP AS THIS TREE'S.
YOUR TREE!
THE QUEST...IT WAS TO FIND OUR PLACE...TO KNOW WHO WE ARE.
ALL OF US WHO WANTED TO, WE FOUND THE STARHOME--
--BECAUSE OF YOU!
I LIVE THERE. AND TIMMAIN, MOTHER OF ALL WOLFRIDERS... SHE'S MY LIFEMATE!
BUT YOU KNOW THAT. EVEN THOUGH HER SKIN'S NOT YOUR SKIN--
--AND EVEN THOUGH IT'S HARD TO UNDERSTAND HOW, OR WHY--
--YOU AND SHE ARE BOTH TAM!
WHEN SHE AND I RECOGNIZED, IT FELT JUST LIKE WHEN YOU AND I...
BUT RECOGNITION, FOR US BROTHERS, WASN'T ABOUT CUBS! IT COULDN'T BE!
WE COULD NEVER HAVE ALL OF EACH OTHER.
YOUR "HUM" WAS ALWAYS HIGHER THAN MINE!
YOU HAD SO MANY DUTIES. AND I PESTERED YOU WITH JOKES AND PRANKS.
I BIT YOU...HIT YOU...PUSHED YOU BECAUSE--
--I LOVE YOU!
AND I WAS AFRAID... ALWAYS AFRAID--
--I'D LOSE YOU.

TAM...FOR EVERY TIME I WASN'T THERE FOR YOU--
--I'M SORRY!
GASP!
THE LODESTONE!
TAM! YOU'RE HERE...ALL AROUND ME!
HIT. HUG. SAME.
LOVE YOU, FAHR.
YOU MEAN... I DID HELP?

OOOOOH! IT'S MY DREAM! THE VISION I SHARED IN PIKE'S DREAM-GAME!
STARS! SO BIG AND BRIGHT THEY DON'T SEEM REAL!
THEY'RE-- THEY'RE GOING AWAY! I DON'T WANT THEM TO!
PLEASE! I WANT TO GO, TOO!
:GASP!: ONE STAR--
--STAYS WITH ME!
IT'S YOU!
HA HA HA HA! CUTTER! IT'S YOU!
PROMISED I'D FLY WITH YOU, DIDN'T I?

WOA! I'M "GOING OUT"!
FIRST TIME!
FIRST TIME! HA HA HAH!
SO THIS IS WHAT IT FEELS LIKE!
HA HA HA!
FREE! GLAD! NO MORE "WHY"!
WHAT YOU WANTED FOR ALL OF US--HAPPINESS AND PEACE--IS IT LIKE THAT FOR YOU?
ALWAYS...IN ALL WAYS!

BUT WHERE DO YOU FIND REST IN A VASTDEEP SEA THAT HAS NO SHORE?
OR A DESERT EXPANSE BOUNDED BY NO MOUNTAINS?
OR AN OPEN PLAIN THAT STRETCHES 'TIL FOREVER?
WHERE DO YOU REST, NOW, IN THE GREAT ALL THAT IS, WHERE ALL THE SUNS AND MOONS AND STARHOMES FLOAT--

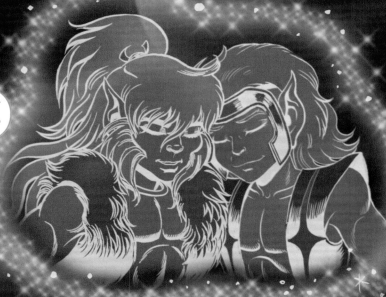

--WHERE **EVERYTHING'S** *ALIVE, FLESH AND SPIRIT*--

--*SWIMMING, CIRCLING, ALWAYS MAKING NEW THREADS IN THE* **SCROLL OF COLORS?**

*I REST IN* **YOU.** *THOSE WHO* **HAVE** *SKINS CAN'T* **KNOW**--

--*HOW MUCH THAT MEANS TO THOSE WHO* **DON'T.**

:GASP!: NO! TOO SOON!
I'M BACK! BACK IN MY OWN SKIN!
BUT YOU CAN'T EVER COME BACK TO YOURS...!
OH, CUTTER! CUTTER!
I MISS YOU! :SOB SOB:
THE CLEANSING TEARS FALL AS THEY MUST. FOR A BROKEN HEART IS THIS QUEST'S ULTIMATE PRIZE.
OOOO! STARGLOW HIGHTHING CRY-CRY!
LET HIM BE, THISTLECAP. LET HIM BE.
PERHAPS NOT AS INTENDED, BROKEN WHEELS GET MENDED AND BROKEN HEARTS HEAL LARGER FOR THE BREAKING. LOVING IS ALWAYS. AND LIVING IS ALWAYS. EACH FEARLESS BREATH WE TAKE IS WORTH THE TAKING.

LATER...
≈SIGH≈ STILL FEEL YOU...WRAPPED ALL AROUND ME LIKE A BLANKET.
HMMM? OH, THAT'S RIGHT.
IN MY DREAM THE BLANKET CHANGES INTO--
--TIMMAIN!
THE DREAM, BELOVED--IT TOLD ME EVERY-THING!
I--I JUST DIDN'T WANT TO SEE!
YOU BELONG--
--HERE, IN MY OWN SKIN--
--WHERE YOU CAN COME REST ANY TIME YOU WANT.
≈SIGH≈ YOU'RE GOING! THE DREAM'S ENDING.
I KNOW! THE LAST THING I'LL SEE IS--
--MY OLD WOLF-FRIEND!
BUT WHY? WHY DO I SEE YOU, STARJUMPER?
FADING, CUTTER'S SPIRIT-VOICE ANSWERS THE QUESTION WITH A QUESTION...
WHAT AM I?
YOU...
YOU'RE DEAD!

AND THEN ONE LAST, PARTING CARESS...
BUT NOT FINISHED!
NO...NOT FINISHED.
YES! I GAVE IT TO YOU!
KEEP IT. KEEP IT
IT'S NOT FINISHED! IT'S--
--PERFECT!
PERFECT!
EH?!
AHA! YOU'RE BACK, YOU ELF-SCUM, AFTE EIGHTS UPON EIGHTS UPON EIGHTS!
BY GUTTLEKRAW'S SHACKLES! WHAT DID YOU DO WITH MY DAUGHTER?!

WENDY PINI
©21

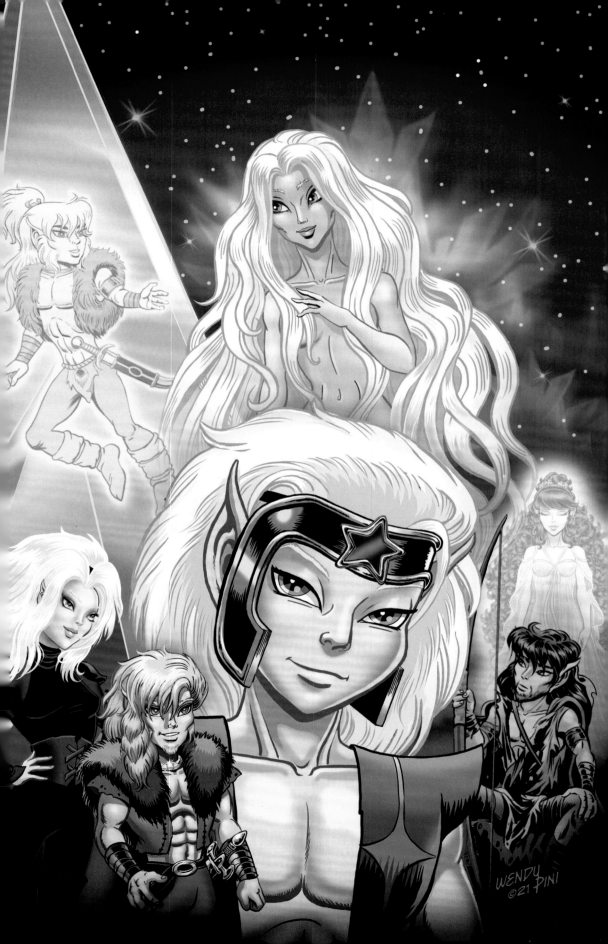

KING PICKNOSE IS ONE UPSET TROLL...AND HE'S BEEN UPSET FOR A VERY LONG TIME.
ELVES KIDNAPPED OUR PRINCESS! AVENGE HER! GET CUTTER'S WHELP!
HE HAS NO MAGIC! TAKE HIM PRISONER!
AYE, GREAT RULER!
YAAARGH!
TAKE ME?!
EH HEH HEH
NASTYBAD DIG-DIGS!
YOU CAN HAVE ME!
HA HA HAH!

GET 'IM!
WHISSH
KNOCK 'IM OUT!
KA-WHOPP
BWOMP
HEY! DID YOU LUMPS FORGET TROLLS AND ELVES--
--DON'T BASH EACH OTHER'S SKULLS ANYMORE?
AYOOOOAH! CUTTER HIMSELF COULDN'T DO BETTER!
MAKES ME WANNA JOIN IN!
NO YOU DON'T!
smack
YOU'RE NOT GETTING THIS SWORD BACK!
SPOOOT!
POOT-POOT-POOT!
GNURRSH!
PHAUGH!

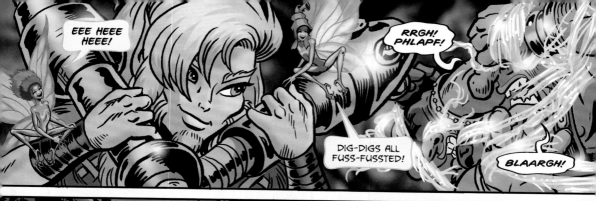

EEE HEEE HEEE!

RRGH! PHLAPF!

DIG-DIGS ALL FUSS-FUSSTED!

BLAARGH!

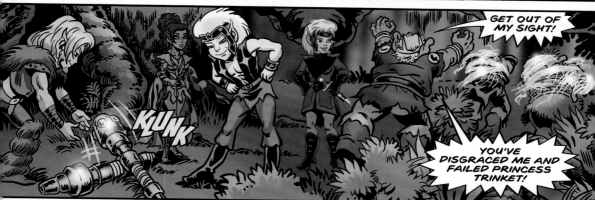

GET OUT OF MY SIGHT!

KLUNK

YOU'VE DISGRACED ME AND FAILED PRINCESS TRINKET!

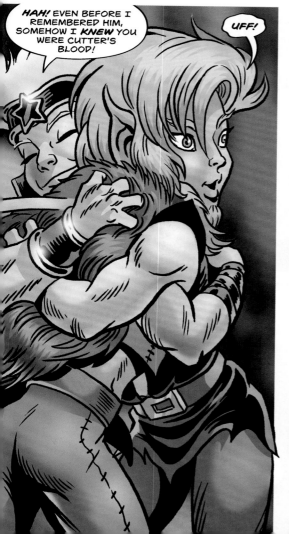

HAH! EVEN BEFORE I REMEMBERED HIM, SOMEHOW I KNEW YOU WERE CUTTER'S BLOOD!

UFF!

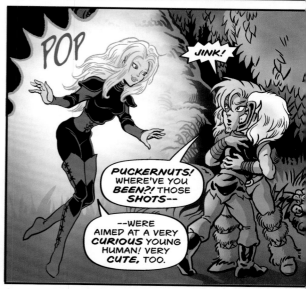

POP

JINK!

PUCKERNUTS! WHERE'VE YOU BEEN?! THOSE SHOTS--

--WERE AIMED AT A VERY CURIOUS YOUNG HUMAN! VERY CUTE, TOO.

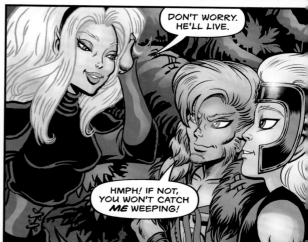

DON'T WORRY. HE'LL LIVE.

HMPH! IF NOT, YOU WON'T CATCH ME WEEPING!

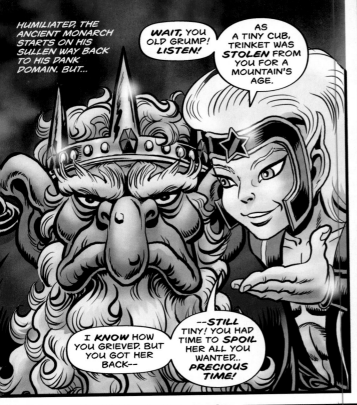

WAIT, YOU OLD GRUMP! *LISTEN!*

AS A TINY CUB, TRINKET WAS *STOLEN* FROM YOU FOR A MOUNTAIN'S AGE.

*I KNOW* HOW YOU GRIEVED. BUT YOU GOT HER BACK--

--STILL TINY! YOU HAD TIME TO *SPOIL* HER ALL YOU WANTED... *PRECIOUS TIME!*

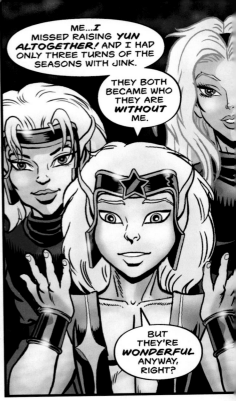

ME...*I* MISSED RAISING *YUN ALTOGETHER!* AND I HAD ONLY THREE TURNS OF THE SEASONS WITH JINK.

THEY BOTH BECAME WHO THEY ARE *WITHOUT* ME.

BUT THEY'RE *WONDERFUL* ANYWAY, RIGHT?

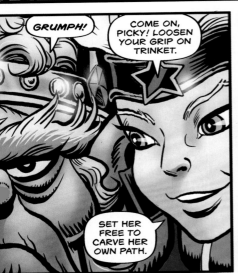

*GRUMPH!*

COME ON, PICKY! LOOSEN YOUR GRIP ON TRINKET.

SET HER FREE TO CARVE HER OWN PATH.

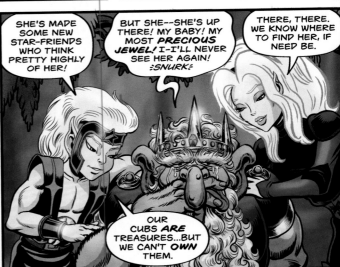

SHE'S MADE SOME NEW STAR-FRIENDS WHO THINK PRETTY HIGHLY OF HER!

BUT SHE--SHE'S UP THERE! MY BABY! MY MOST *PRECIOUS JEWEL!* I-I'LL NEVER SEE HER AGAIN! =SNURK=

THERE, THERE. WE KNOW WHERE TO FIND HER, IF NEED BE.

OUR CUBS *ARE* TREASURES...BUT WE CAN'T *OWN* THEM.

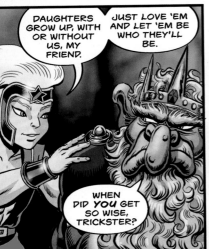

DAUGHTERS GROW UP, WITH OR WITHOUT US, MY FRIEND.

JUST LOVE 'EM AND LET 'EM BE WHO THEY'LL BE.

WHEN DID *YOU* GET SO WISE, TRICKSTER?

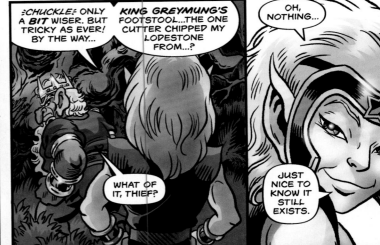

=CHUCKLE= ONLY A *BIT* WISER. BUT TRICKY AS EVER! BY THE WAY...

*KING GREYMUNG'S* FOOTSTOOL...THE ONE CUTTER CHIPPED MY LODESTONE FROM...?

WHAT OF IT, THIEF?

OH, NOTHING...

JUST NICE TO KNOW IT STILL EXISTS.

:SSIPP: DOES THE WATER ON THE **STARHOME** TASTE LIKE THIS?

NOT EVEN THE FRESHEST SPRING THERE COMES CLOSE!

:HEH: I THINK WHAT YOU **REALLY** MEAN IS--

--YOU STILL **LOVE** THE HOLT...AND YOU **MISS** IT.

YOU'RE SO LIKE **HIM!** BUT YOU HAVE **LEETAH'S** EYES.

AND THEY TELL ME YOU'VE SEEN A **LOT.**

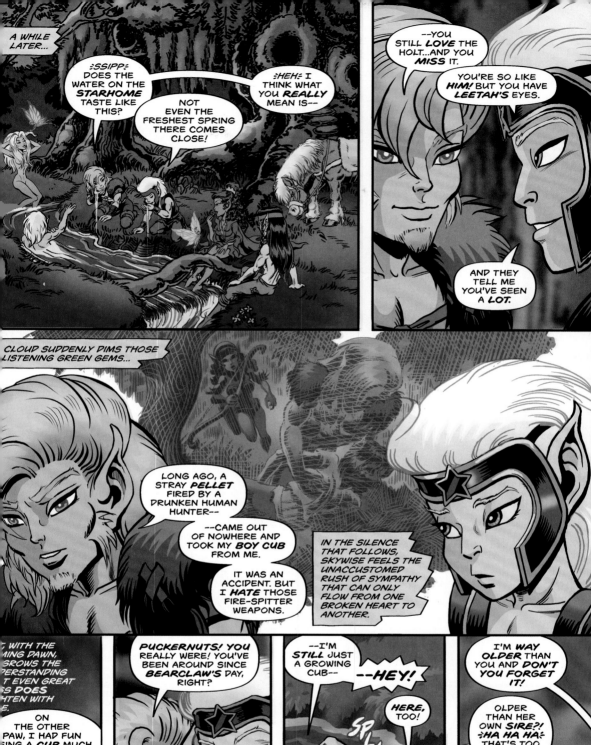

CLOUD SUDDENLY DIMS THOSE LISTENING GREEN GEMS...

LONG AGO, A STRAY **PELLET** FIRED BY A DRUNKEN HUMAN HUNTER--

--CAME OUT OF NOWHERE AND TOOK MY **BOY CUB** FROM ME.

IT WAS AN ACCIDENT. BUT I **HATE** THOSE FIRE-SPITTER WEAPONS.

IN THE SILENCE THAT FOLLOWS, SKYWISE FEELS THE UNACCUSTOMED RUSH OF SYMPATHY THAT CAN ONLY FLOW FROM ONE BROKEN HEART TO ANOTHER.

, WITH THE MING DAWN, ROWS THE PERSTANDING T EVEN GREAT S **DOES** TEN WITH E.

ON THE OTHER PAW, I HAD FUN EING A **CUB** MUCH LONGER THAN TTER. HIS DUTIES STARTED **TOO EARLY.**

HAT THEY D. I WAS THERE.

PUCKERNUTS! YOU REALLY WERE! YOU'VE BEEN AROUND SINCE **BEARCLAW'S** DAY, RIGHT?

:HEH HEH: YET, ON THE STARHOME--

--I'M **STILL** JUST A GROWING CUB--

**--HEY!**

HERE, TOO!

SPLISH

I'M **WAY OLDER** THAN YOU AND **DON'T YOU FORGET IT!**

OLDER THAN HER OWN **SIRE?!** :HA HA HA: THAT'S TOO MUCH FOR ME!

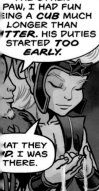
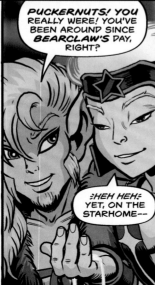
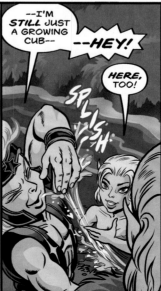
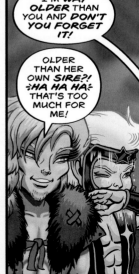

WHILE JINK AND YUN BRING THEIR COMPACTED PODS OUT FROM HIDING...
TELL MENDER IT FALLS TO HIM, FOR NOW, TO DO THE WORK OF TWO HEALERS.
MOTHER, IT'S STILL A LONG WAY.
I DON'T LIKE YOU TRAVELING ANYWHERE NEAR HUMANS OR THEIR STINKING METAL WAGONS AND WEAPONS!
NOW, NOW. THERE'S NOT A HIDDEN PATH OR SECRET BYWAY THAT DRE-AHN DOESN'T KNOW.
I COULDN'T BE IN SAFER HANDS.
OWL PELLETS! YOU COULD LET YUN AND JINK POD-FL YOU STRAIGHT TO THE ROOTLESS ONES' DELL!
AH NO! I HAVE OTHER TASKS FOR THEM.
WHAT, MOTHER OF MEMORY?
JINK... SKYWISE... PLEASE TAKE THIS WILLFUL CUB BACK TO WHERE YOU FOUND HIM.
GROWL
AND YUN, YOU MUST FLY TO THE WOLFRIDERS. WHAT WITH BEING DRIVEN FAR FROM THE HOLT, PERHAPS EVEN BEYOND THE INSECT TRIBES' PROTECTION--
AYE!
I'M BETTING ALL THIS WORLD'S ELVES COULD USE SOME SWIFT GETTING ABOUT, JUST NOW.
JINK...WHEN YOU AND I SET OFF TO FIND FATHER, I HADN'T A GLIMMER THAT SO MUCH TIME WOULD PASS HERE.
TAKE SKYWISE BACK TO THE STARHOME, LITTLE SISTER.
I'M GOING TO STAY.
THISTLECAP STAY TOO!
GOOD, MY TINY FRIEND! PROTECT T WOLFRIDERS.

HE NEW DAY'S LIGHT, AFTER ALL FAREWELLS
E BEEN MADE, LEETAH AND SKYWISE SHARE
T ONLY THEY CAN SHARE.
DOES HE...DOES HE COME ANY TIME YOU CALL?
NO.
...
NOT EVEN FOR YOU?!
WHENEVER HE COMES TO ME, I AM CONTENT.
IT MAY SEEM THAT THEY ABANDON US, SKYWISE.
BUT SPIRITS ARE FREE...FREE IN WAYS WE CAN ONLY BEGIN TO KNOW.
NO MATTER HOW WE LONG FOR THEIR COMPANY, WE MUST NEVER TRY TO COMMAND THEM OR BEG THEM TO STAY--
--OR HOLD THEM PRISONER.
IT'S WRONG.
AND SO...
MOTHER...
SHE'S ON A QUEST OF HER OWN, NOW.
MOMENTS LATER, JINK AND YUN'S PODS, LIKE TWO BLAZING COMETS, STREAK TO THEIR SEPARATE DESTINATIONS--

--NOT UNNOTICED BY PAR TOLFSSON AND HIS CAPTORS NEAR THE EDGE OF THE INSECT TRIBES' SACRED TERRITORY.
AM I UNDER ARREST?
NO. YOU'LL BE ESCORTED BACK ACROSS THE BORDER.
RUM TATTA TUM...TUM TUM...RUM TATTA TUM...TUM T
BUT KEEP IN MIND--
--MY SCOUTS HAVE ORDERS TO SHOOT YOU DEAD, NO QUESTIONS ASKED, IF YOU EVER TRESPASS AGAIN.
AND THAT'D BE A SHAME. A CURIOUS MIND'S A GOOD THING...SO LONG AS IT'S RESPECTFUL.
I KNOW WHAT I SAW, QUEEN BEE.
A BEAUTIFUL SILHOUETTE, MOVING TOO FAST TO SEE CLEARLY--
--BUT I SAW IT! AND IT WASN'T HUMAN!
NO ONE CAN TELL ME I'M WRONG!
WRONG ABOUT WHAT, GRUB? I DIDN'T SEE ANYTHING. YOU GOT PROOF? A PHOTOGRAPH, MAYBE?
YOU KNOW I DON'T.
THEY WON'T BELIEVE YOU ON YOUR SIDE OF THE BORDER.
THAT'S HOW THE INSECT TRIBES LIKE IT. THAT'S HOW IT HAS TO BE.
WE'LL SEE, ZAZAPAT IKOPEK...
YEAH, I KNOW, GRUB. YOU WON'T BE CONTENT WITH JUST THIS. YOU'LL BE A STICKER IN MY BUTT LONG AS I LIVE--

"--MAYBE LONGER."
Caw! Caw! Caw!
HUNH?!
INSIDE THE NEWLY ARRIVED POD--
--GOLDRUFF IS EAGER TO GREET HIS WAITING FRIENDS. BUT A TOUCH FROM SKYWISE STAYS HIM.
YOU'RE SURE THE WOLFRIDERS ARE ALL RIGHT?
YOUR CHIEF-SISTER, EMBER...SHE'S GOT IT ALL IN HAND?
WILL THEY EVER RECLAIM FATHER TREE HOLT?
ANCED BY THE 'S POWERFUL A--
LOCK-SEND S SKYWISE THAT HAS ALLEN THE FRIDERS CE CUTTER'S TH.
OH! OH STARS!
THE REST HAS YET TO BE LIVED!
HEN, AS ELFIN SIRE AND DAUGHTER ENTLY SEND GOLDRUFF AND HISTLECAP FLOATING OUTSIDE...
FARE WELL, STARGAZER! TAKE CARE, LOVELY JINK!
NOKKAH! BLACKWING! BENT BEAK!
WHAT TOOK YOU, SHAGBACK MEAT?
WHAT TOOK ME?! I'VE NOT BEEN GONE ONE FULL NIGHT!
SO... WHAT TOOK YOU?!
GRRRR!
SQUAWK!

TELL YOU ONCE WE'RE HEADED BACK TO THE TRIBE.
RIGHT NOW, SKYWISE IS HEADED STRAIGHT FOR THE STARHOME TO BE WITH HIS LIFEMATE, *TIMMAIN.*
BUT HE'LL *RETURN,* HE AND JINK. THEY CAN GO ANYWHERE... ANYTIME.
*SHE* CAN GO TO THE *FIRE PIT!*
AND YOU'RE *NOT* GETTING THIS *CRYSTAL* OF HERS BACK, EITHER!
YOU'RE RIGHT. I'VE GO A *BETTER* IDEA!
SNIP
HEY!
SKYWISE! WAIT!
YOU LEFT YOUR *LODESTONE* WITH MY FATHER.
TAKE *TH* INSTEAD

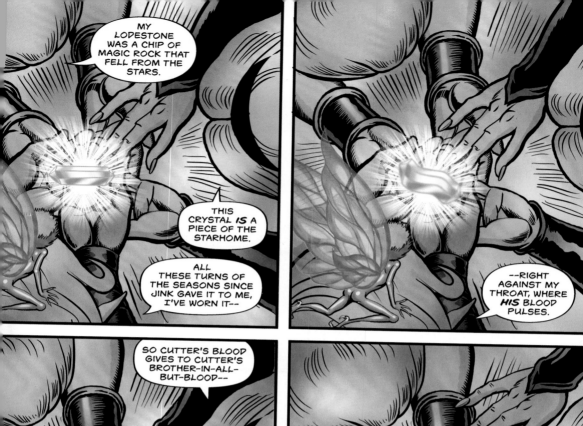

MY LODESTONE WAS A CHIP OF MAGIC ROCK THAT FELL FROM THE STARS.

THIS CRYSTAL *IS* A PIECE OF THE STARHOME.

ALL THESE TURNS OF THE SEASONS SINCE JINK GAVE IT TO ME, I'VE WORN IT--

--RIGHT AGAINST MY THROAT, WHERE *HIS* BLOOD PULSES.

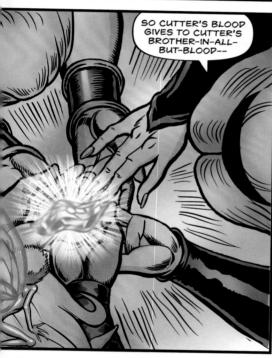

SO CUTTER'S BLOOD GIVES TO CUTTER'S BROTHER-IN-ALL-BUT-BLOOD--

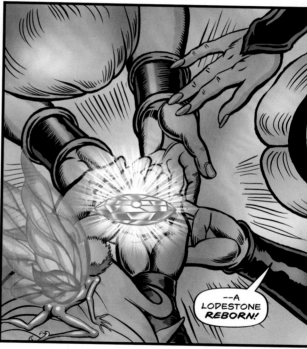

--A LODESTONE *REBORN!*

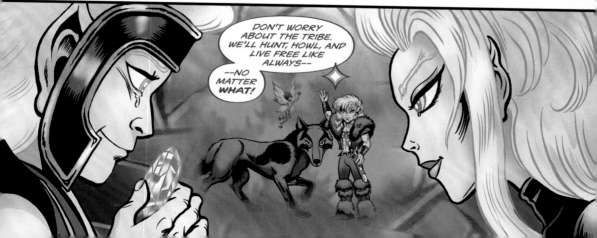

DON'T WORRY ABOUT THE TRIBE. WE'LL HUNT, HOWL, AND LIVE FREE LIKE ALWAYS--

--NO MATTER *WHAT!*

HOW LONG TO REACH THE STARHOME? A BLINK? AN ETERNITY? BOTH?
SKYWISE, IN HIGH ONE FORM, DELIGHTS IN THE OPEN SENDINGS OF HIS FELLOW ELVES WHO HAVE NOT, HIS EYES SEE WITH JOY, EVER FORGOTTEN HIM.
THEN ON TO SUNSTREAM, CUTTER'S FIRSTBORN SON, SOON TO BE A FATHER AGAIN--
--WHO WILL PASS ON THE KNOWLEDGE OF GOLDRUFF, HIS OWN MORTAL BROTHER, WHO CARRIES ON THE WOLFRIDERS' WAY IN GRAND STYLE.
AND, TO HIS RELIEF, SKYWISE DOES SEE IN THOSE FAMILIAR, SHARP FEATURES THAT THERE IS NO REPROACH FOR HIS LEAVING FAMILY AND FRIENDS SO ABRUPTLY.
YOU KNOW.
YES. YOUR EYES...
...THEY'RE DEEPER THAN BEFORE. THEY SHOW MORE OF WHAT'S INSIDE YOU.

ONG THE MANY AFFECTIONATE UNIONS, THE RETURNED AVELER ESPECIALLY SEEKS OUT E LABYRINTHINE TROLL KINGDOM NEATH PALACE CITY, WHERE REGALES THE PERPETUALLY FENDED OLD MAGGOTY--
--WITH TALES OF TRINKET AND HER HOSPITABLE, STAR-BORN COUSINS, THE SCULPERS.
OWARD LATE AFTERNOON, WHEN HERE CAN BE NO MORE DELAY THE JOURNEY THAT HAS ROUGHT HIM TO THIS MOMENT...
SHE AWAITS YOU IN THE BOWER BEYOND STRONGBOW'S WOODS.
NOW HIS IS A FACE I'D LIKE TO SEE BEFORE...
WE KNOW.
THANKS, VENKA.
YOU ADE ROOM FOR HIM.
AND YOU... OU'RE TALKING RE THAN I'VE EVER ARD! ARE YOU AND MOONSHADE--?
IT TOOK TIME. BUT WE DANCE OFTEN NOW.
NOT THAT SHE APPROVES ANY MORE THAN BEFORE OF THE CONDITION OF MY LEATHERS.
HERE, "HIGH ONE." KEPT FOR YOU. WHATEVER SHAPE YOU TAKE, DON'T EVER FORGET WHERE WE CAME FROM.
NEVER!

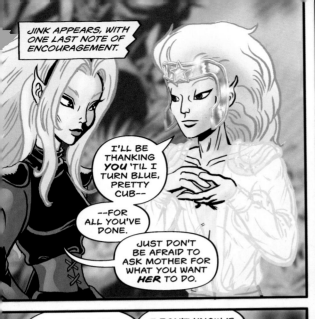

JINK APPEARS, WITH ONE LAST NOTE OF ENCOURAGEMENT.

I'LL BE THANKING *YOU* 'TIL I TURN BLUE, PRETTY CUB--

--FOR ALL YOU'VE DONE. JUST DON'T BE AFRAID TO ASK MOTHER FOR WHAT YOU WANT *HER* TO DO.

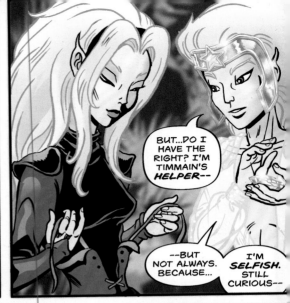

BUT...DO I HAVE THE RIGHT? I'M TIMMAIN'S *HELPER*--

--BUT NOT ALWAYS. BECAUSE...

I'M *SELFISH*. STILL CURIOUS--

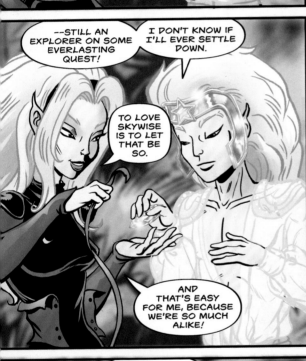

--STILL AN EXPLORER ON SOME EVERLASTING QUEST!

I DON'T KNOW IF I'LL EVER SETTLE DOWN.

TO LOVE SKYWISE IS TO LET THAT BE SO.

AND THAT'S EASY FOR ME, BECAUSE WE'RE SO MUCH ALIKE!

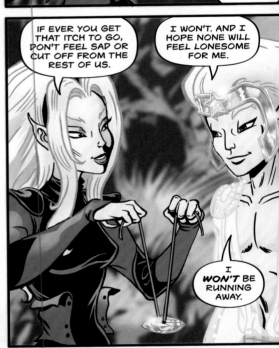

IF EVER YOU GET THAT ITCH TO GO, DON'T FEEL SAD OR CUT OFF FROM THE REST OF US.

I WON'T. AND I HOPE NONE WILL FEEL LONESOME FOR ME.

I *WON'T* BE RUNNING AWAY.

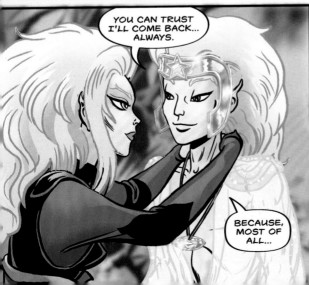

YOU CAN TRUST I'LL COME BACK... ALWAYS.

BECAUSE, MOST OF ALL...

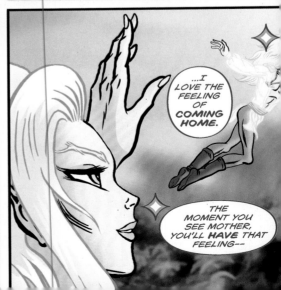

...I LOVE THE FEELING OF *COMING HOME*.

THE MOMENT YOU SEE MOTHER, YOU'LL *HAVE* THAT FEELING--

--AND YOU'LL KNOW WHAT TO SAY."
FAHR!
:SIGH:
DON'T EVER TAKE CUTTER'S SHAPE AGAIN. JUST BE YOU!
I CANNOT BE HIM. BUT I DO STILL FOLLOW HIM AS I DID ON THE WORLD OF TWO MOONS.
HE DOES NOT MIND.
HE'S YOUR OTHER SELF! SO...YOU KNOW WHAT HAPPENED IN THE FATHER TREE.
BUT FOR ALL YOU'VE LEARNED FROM HIM--
"--DID YOU EVER LEARN THE WARMTH OF HIS HEART...HIS SIMPLE, EASY WAY OF LOVING?
"MORE THAN ANYTHING, LIFEMATE, I WANT THAT!"
"I NEED THAT...FROM YOU!"

TIMMAIN, FIRSTCOMER, HIGHEST OF **ALL** HIGH ONES, MOTHER OF ALL WOLFRIDERS--
--MOTHER OF OUR MAGNIFICENT JINK...SHARED SOUL OF MY HEART'S DEAREST FRIEND...
YOU BROUGHT A DROP OF CUTTER'S BLOOD **HERE** WITH YOU! IT SLEEPS IN YOUR VEINS **NOW!**
A **GIFT,** YOU SAID, TO BE GRANTED ANY HIGH ONE WHO CHOOSES TO KNOW OLD AGE AND DEATH.
BUT THAT TINY DROP ALSO HOLDS ALL THE TENDERNESS...THE FRIENDSHIP...THE **UNDERSTANDING** I'VE MISSED AND MOURNED!

YOU ASK FOR CUTTER'S MORTAL WARMTH...THE ONE THING I KNOW NOT HOW TO GIVE.
THROUGH HIM CAME THE LESSON OF PAIN, MINE TO LEARN AND EMBRACE...BUT HIS TO TRULY LIVE.
BECAUSE OF HIM, I COULD STUDY THE SCROLL OF COLORS IN THE QUIET SECLUSION OF THE PALACE--
--OR VENTURE OUT, SHAPED AS WOLF OR HIGH ONE, TO JOIN THE QUEST AT WILL.
HE LIVED AND DIED BY THE GREATNESS OF HIS HEART AND THE WOLFSONG IN HIS BLOOD. BUT I--
FIND IT! DRAW ON ALL THE FIERY WOLF SENSE IT HOLDS!
CUTTER'S WOLFRIDER SON--YOUR SON, GOLDRUFF--
--GAVE THIS TO ME. AND IT FELT ALMOST AS IF MY LONG-GONE WOLF BLOOD WAS RESTORED! USE IT TO FEEL A WOLFRIDER'S HUM...ALL THE WAY BACK TO A WOLF'S!

"PLEASE...FOR ME, LIFEMATE, CALL UP INSIDE YOU THE WARMTH OF LIVING, FIGHTING, HUNTING AND LOVING IN THE 'NOW'!"
TO GO FROM HAVING ENDURED SO LONG...SEEN SO MUCH...CARRIED SO MANY MEMORIES THAT SIMPLE FEELING HAS GONE OUT OF THEM--
--TO BEING A TRUE FRIEND...A TRUE LIFEMATE...TO SKYWISE THE STARGAZER--
YES! LET THE AUSTERE HIGH ONE RETREAT...AND THE HOT-BLOODED WOLF SPIRIT COME FORTH! THE FEROCITY...
THE WISDOM...
THE "NOW" OF WOLF THOUGHT...

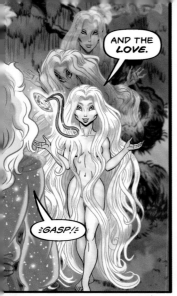

AND THE **LOVE**.

:GASP!:

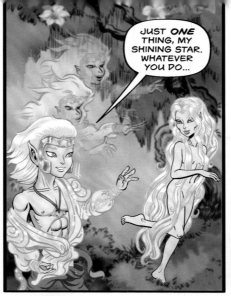

JUST **ONE** THING, MY SHINING STAR. WHATEVER YOU DO...

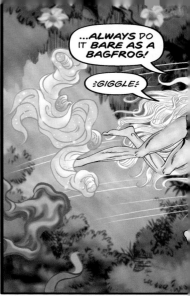

...ALWAYS DO IT **BARE** AS A **BAGFROG!**

:GIGGLE:

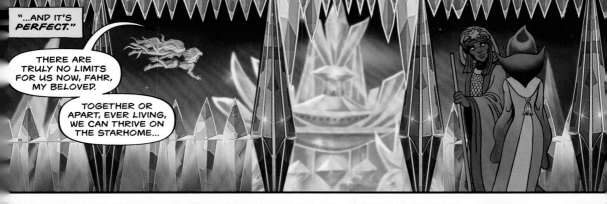

THERE ARE **MANY** WORLDS, STRONGBOW, FULL OF THINGS THAT ARE BORN AND LIVE AND DIE IN THEIR OWN WAYS.

MAYBE SO. I SUPPOSE OUR KIND HAS VISITED...AND WILL GO RIGHT ON VISITING...THOSE PLACES.

BUT ME...WELL, CUTTER SAID IT BEST.

"THERE'S MY SKIN AND THERE'S ME. AND WHEN I DIE, THERE'LL JUST BE ME."

ME AND THESE WOODS. THAT'S ALL *I* NEED...

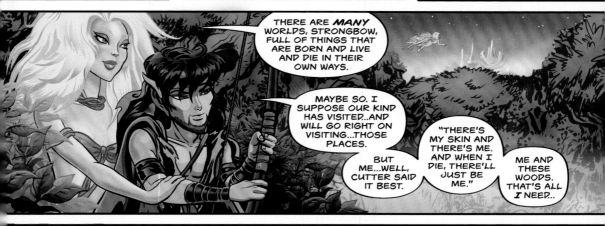

"...AND IT'S **PERFECT.**"

THERE ARE TRULY NO LIMITS FOR US NOW, FAHR, MY BELOVED.

TOGETHER OR APART, EVER LIVING, WE CAN THRIVE ON THE STARHOME...

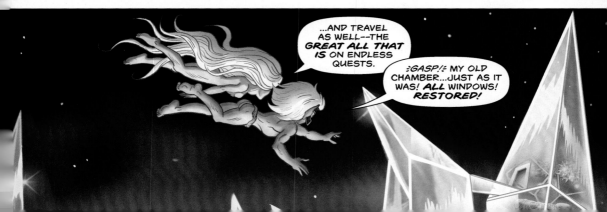

...AND TRAVEL AS WELL--THE **GREAT ALL THAT IS** ON ENDLESS QUESTS.

:GASP!: MY OLD CHAMBER...JUST AS IT WAS! **ALL** WINDOWS! **RESTORED!**

EVERYTHING I COULD EVER WANT IS RIGHT HERE IN MY ARMS.
YOU'RE MY VERY OWN CANDLE--BRIGHTER THAN ANY OTHER--TO GUIDE ME HOME.
WHEREVER I AM, FAHR, YOU ARE HOME.
BUT NOW...I'M SLEEPY.
YOU?! YOU NEVER SLEEP!
ALL I WANT IS TO CURL UP WITH YOU--
--AND NAP LIKE TWO WOLVES IN THEIR DEN.
TELL ME, BELOVED, IN YOUR OWN TRAVELS AMONG THE STARS.
DID YOU EVER NOTICE--
--HOW THEY SEEM SO MUCH FURTHER APART AND FARTHER AWAY--
--THAN THEY LOOK WHEN YOU JUST...
...LEAN BACK?
ONWARD--WITHOUT END.

WENDY PINI ©21

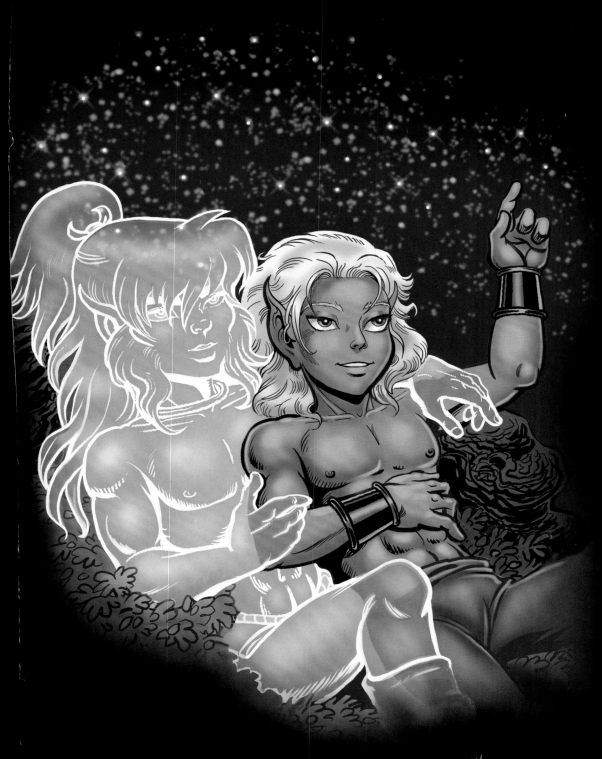

# STARGAZER ON THE RUN
by Richard Pini

When he gets his memory wiped and feels something's wrong or missing, is Skywise going into space (isolation) to run away, or to reflect (go introspective)? My thought is, this is not an either/or question—one or the other—but rather a case of one evolving into the other.

It's like when I take a drive to nowhere when my brain is full and buzzing and useless. I'm not running away, per se, from anything. I need a break, I need to hit the "pause" button and stop trying to think and solve. Just let the wind and the quiet and the isolation blow through my skull and cool things down. And when I do that, and the mind chatter simmers down, I'm able somehow to find one thread in the knotted-up ball of yarn that I can pull on just a little, and maybe tease it out a bit, and follow that one thread to find a solution (or part of one). And then the Gordian knot isn't quite so complex anymore, and other things start to fall into perspective instead of seeming intractable.

Skywise's—and my—initial impulse may look like running, and in a sense it is. But it's not running **away** from a thing. Rather, it's running **toward** a sense of needing some quiet. Skywise isn't a coward, but he can become overwhelmed—we've seen it before. And as we've said, where can one go that's quieter and more isolated (and potentially overwhelming in those qualities) than the vastness of space? Plus, that destination would make sense, because he's always wanted to explore the stars anyway. Maybe this can become two edged in itself—be careful what you wish for!

It may appear at times that I have sudden epiphanies, but that's not how it works for me (and it's not how it would work for Skywise). What look like realizations are simply the accumulation of a lot of smaller bits of learning or observing or experience that pile up in my brain/memory and then "suddenly" I can see the connections and patterns between and among them. And then there is a rush of "Ah, now this makes sense." Very often, it takes time for that to happen. Sometimes it's unconscious as I go about my daily life. Other times it's the result of a more deliberate effort—a drive to nowhere, a.k.a. "running away"—that gives me the mental and emotional elbow room and time to look at things from a less involved point of view.

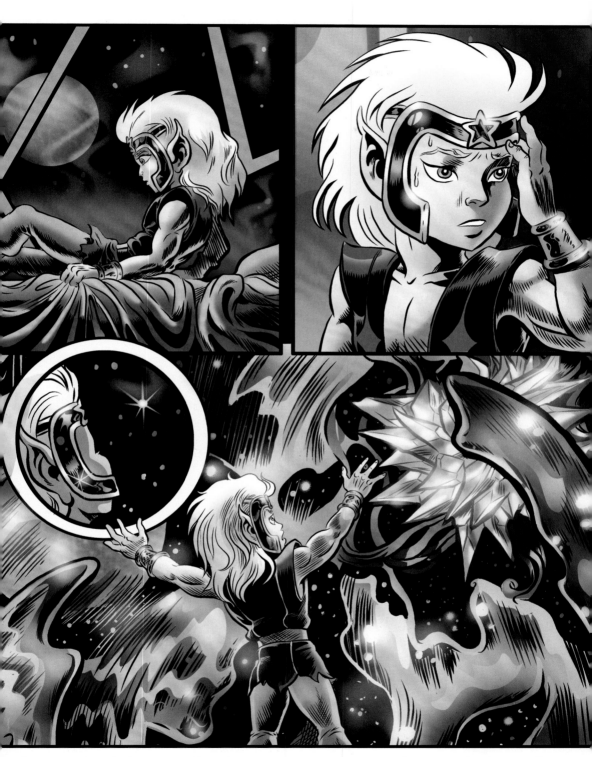

Sometimes the vehicle is an earthbound minivan; sometimes an interstellar pod made of star-stuff. Either way the desire—no, the need—to break loose and try to outrun a chattering mind is a shared connector between reality and fantasy.

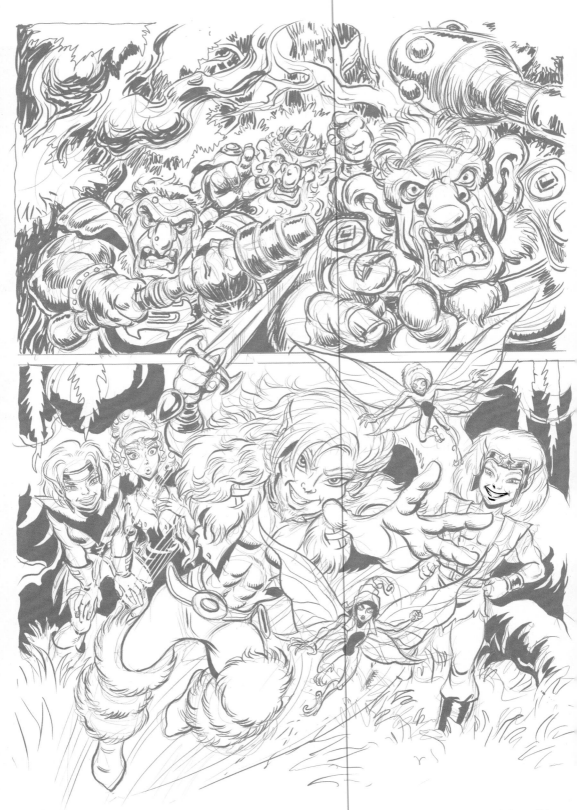

*Wendy's pencils over her blue-line rough layouts. Facing page: Sonny's inks, under which he will lay in the colors, add just the right weight and dimension to the composition. Note the Preservers' lack of wings on the inked page; those will be added as held colors without outlines.*

# Dream Job
by Sonny Strait

We've done some awesome things in *ElfQuest* using Photoshop. Beautiful painterly effects, skies of poetic serenity, weather conditions of any extreme, even crystalline, otherworldly structures with colors that you can feel vibrate in your teeth.

My job as a finisher has been to take whatever Wendy gives me and turn it into *ElfQuest*. Depending on the page, I could be penciling, inking, painting, or even taking a collage of reference photos to blend into Photoshop brilliance.

But occasionally, like the page I worked on last night, Wendy will throw me an old-school, straightforward, fully penciled page she's done for me to ink. This is something we could have done for years before Photoshop came along. I have to say, these are some of my favorite projects.

Honestly, I'd be a happy camper if my whole job was just inking over Wendy's pencils. I learn so much in the process. Even now, over twenty years after she took me on as her apprentice. I'd be in great company too, with the likes of comic greats Joe Staton and John Byrne, who also inked for Wendy.

Ah, well . . . enough daydreaming. Now to color the page I inked last night.

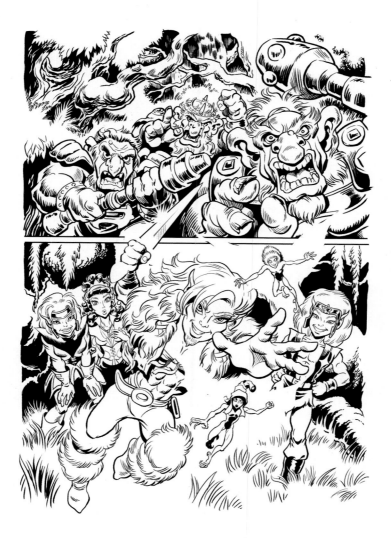

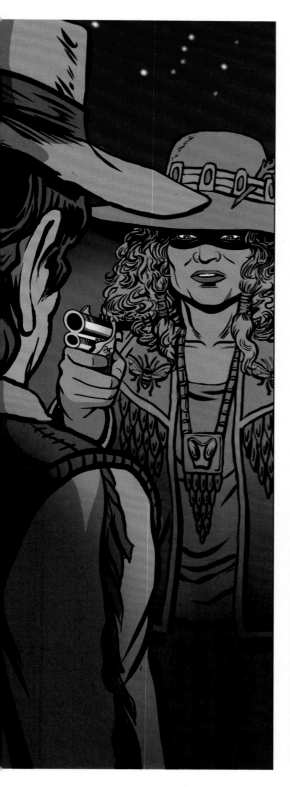

# Shades of Gray
by Wendy Pini

Thoughts for whatever it's worth, just before turning in on a quiet Sunday night . . .

Perhaps it's the current highly polarized political atmosphere, but from time to time I'm struck with the realization that I have no morals. Strong likes and dislikes, attractions and aversions, yes. But I have no beliefs about them. Or, perhaps, better to say no dogmatic value system that holds fast in any and all cases.

I was raised by atheists who sent me to church because it wouldn't look good to the community if they didn't. Church went right over my head. Good and evil, heaven and hell, sin and judgment . . . none of it "took." You see, very early on I learned it's possible to love the imperfect, to stand by it and remain your own person—unless the imperfect proves it really wants to kill you. Then you shut the door and leave.

I've always loved ambiguity—the tarnished hero; the noble, committed villain.

"Will the good guy defeat the bad guy?" is still the basic dramatic question in most pop culture entertainment, but I don't find much value in that. What really excites me is the hero's—or even the villain's—internal struggle, which I liken to the writhing of a butterfly striving to escape from its cocoon. I find more suspense in following a character's personal journey toward whatever transformation awaits them than in any straightforward good-versus-evil scenario.

So, just because the elves in *ElfQuest* treat all living things the best they possibly can, it doesn't make them inherently good. If anything, placing black-and-white judgments on my characters would hobble me as a creator. There are many more interesting twists and possibilities when you wander the Gray Lands.

*Facing page: Queen Bee, head councilwoman of the United Insect Tribes, is a matriarch you do not want to mess with. She looks at the world with a calm, present gaze and a wry sense of humor . . .*

*This page: . . . but disobey the tribal laws she upholds and, even if she likes you, she won't hesitate to kill you. And she won't cry about it afterward, either. A heart she has, but soft it is not.*

Timmain, highest of all High Ones, ancient and timeless, an immortal elfin goddess whose thoughts are impossible to read, whose actions are often confounding and seemingly devoid of empathy.

Timmain, female incarnation of the soul she shares with her mortal descendant and other self, Wolfrider chief Cutter. Through her connection with him she has learned—and is still learning—how to love, to laugh, and to care for others' feelings.

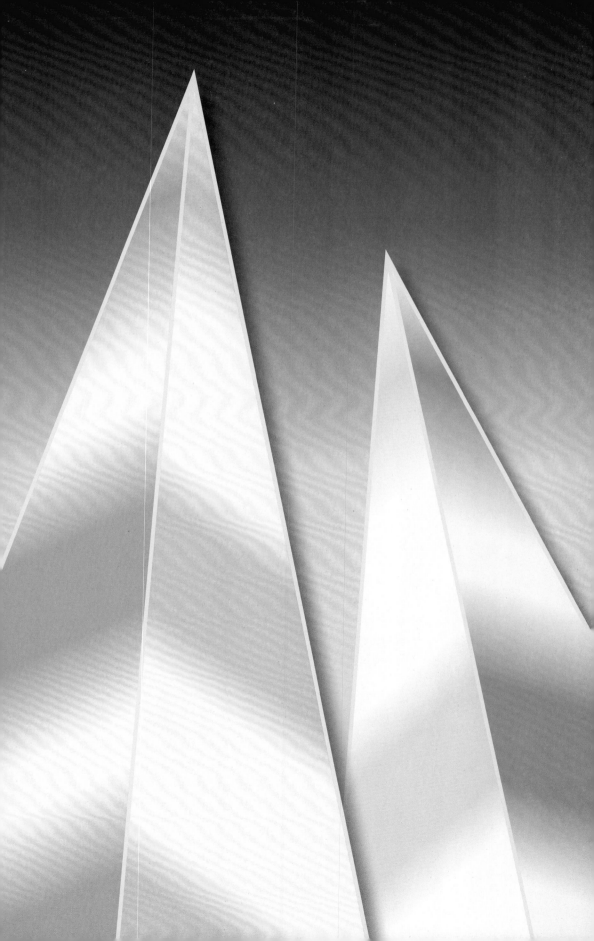

WENDY PINI
©21

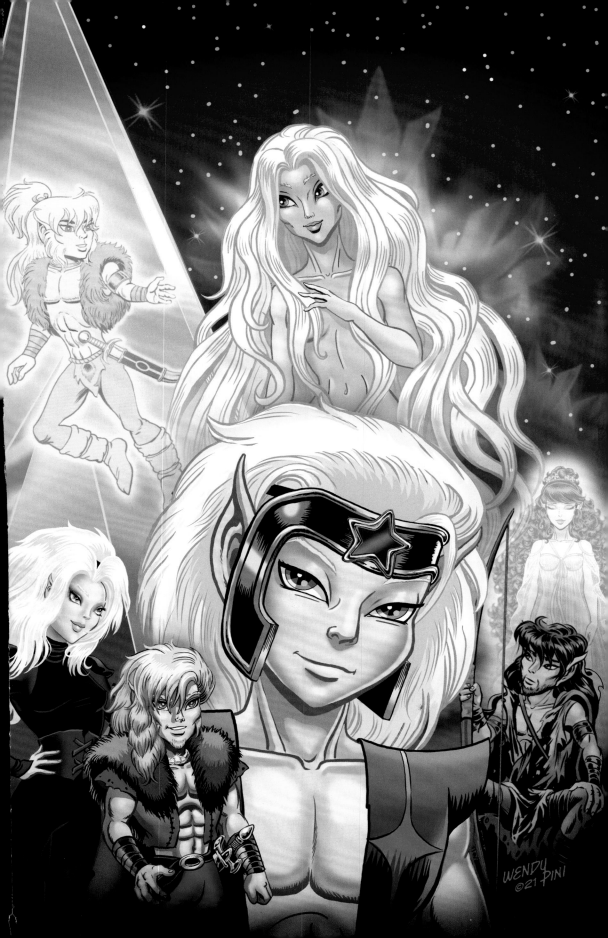

# ELFQUEST®

DISCOVER THE LEGEND OF *ELFQUEST*! ALLIANCES ARE FORGED, ENEMIES DISCOVERED, AND SAVAGE BATTLES FOUGHT IN THIS EPIC FANTASY ADVENTURE, HANDSOMELY PRESENTED BY DARK HORSE BOOKS!

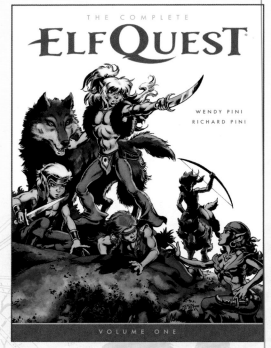

## THE COMPLETE ELFQUEST

**Volume 1: The Original Quest**
978-1-61655-407-1 | $29.99

**Volume 2**
978-1-61655-408-8 | $29.99

**Volume 3**
978-1-50670-080-9 | $29.99

**Volume 4**
978-1-50670-158-5 | $29.99

**Volume 5**
978-1-50670-606-1 | $29.99

**Volume 6**
978-1-50670-607-8 | $29.99

**Volume 7**
978-1-50670-608-5 | $29.99

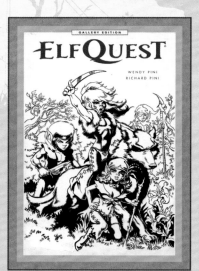

## ELFQUEST: THE ORIGINAL QUEST GALLERY EDITION
978-1-61655-411-8 | $125.00

## ELFQUEST: THE FINAL QUEST

**Volume 1**
978-1-61655-409-5 | $19.99

**Volume 2**
978-1-61655-410-1 | $17.99

**Volume 3**
978-1-50670-138-7 | $19.99

**Volume 4**
978-1-50670-492-0 | $19.99

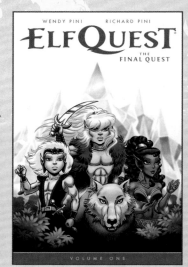

**AVAILABLE AT YOUR LOCAL COMICS SHOP OR BOOKSTORE**
To find a comics shop in your area, visit comicshoplocator.com. For more information or to order direct visit DarkHorse.com

ElfQuest © Warp Graphics, Inc. Dark Horse Books® and the Dark Horse logo are registered trademarks of Dark Horse Comics LLC. All rights reserved. (BL 8050)